Enterprising Ideas for Secondary Schools

enterprising careers

CENTRE FOR STUDIES IN ENTERPRISE, CAREER DEVELOPMENT & WORK

University of Strathclyde
Glasgow

Authors:

Moreen Smith, Development Manager, Enterprising Careers
Jess Duncan, Development Manager, Enterprising Careers

Centre for Studies in Enterprise, Career Development & Work
University of Strathclyde
Jordanhill Campus
Southbrae Drive
Glasgow
G13 1PP
Email: enterprising.careers@strath.ac.uk

© Enterprising Careers, University of Strathclyde, 2007.
   ISBN: 978 1 9007 43 63 1

Foreword

Our young people need to have a clear purpose and a 'can do' attitude to allow them to make the most of any opportunities in a personal, work or community context. They need to be flexible, creative, resourceful and prepared to take the initiative, and it is widely acknowledged that enterprise education can help to foster these skills and attributes.

In the last few years, Scottish initiatives such as National Priorities (SEED 2000), Ambitious Excellent Schools (SEED, 2004), A Curriculum for Excellence (SEED, 2004); Assessment is for Learning (SEED, 2004) and publications such as *Count Us In: Achieving Inclusion in Scottish Schools* (HMIe, 2002); *Improving Scottish Education* (HMIE, 2006) and *The Journey to Excellence* (HMIe, 2006) have embraced much of the philosophy behind enterprise education. It is generally recognised that an enterprising approach to teaching and learning can help to deliver the outcomes hoped for from these initiatives.

The last few years have seen substantial development in enterprise education in secondary schools. Enterprise education is moving from a project-based initiative involving business, social or community events to an overall approach to teaching and learning. Teachers recognise the need to work in an enterprising way - motivating students and ensuring that the curriculum is relevant and purposeful for all.

The materials in this publication reflect much of the good practice which currently exists in our schools. We have drawn on the ideas from many schools across the country. Others are based on good practice that Enterprising Careers staff have encountered in CPD courses in Scotland and elsewhere. While some of these ideas are organised on the basis of subjects, enterprising teachers will see that they are adaptable and can be used in a variety of contexts. Others are presented as cross-curricular or whole school examples and may be used in a variety of ways. Additional sections containing background information and toolkits are designed to provide support with assessment and evaluation, and are largely drawn from techniques and approaches used in evaluation by Enterprising Careers.

So - we hope that there is something in the book for everyone, and that it will be a support to teachers as they seek to meet the needs of their pupils!

Linda Brownlow
Co-director
Centre for Studies in Enterprise, Career Development and Work

Acknowledgements

We would like to thank the many schools and teachers who have submitted their creative ideas to share good practice and make this work more relevant for their colleagues whilst meeting the current curriculum structure in our schools. We know that there are many fantastic ideas out there to share nationally, but can only provide so much in this, our first edition. Sharing good practice is the most effective way to increase the pace of culture change. We should support one another to enable us to move forward in our own learning.

We greatly appreciate the support received so far and wish you continued success in making schools the purposeful places they should be, supporting and working with not only the students who are our first concern, but also their families, businesses and local communities - as we are all in this together to make a Smart, Successful Scotland.

Our sincere thanks to the following schools and local authorities for contributing to this resource. While it was not possible to use all of the material, we are grateful to you for your contributions.

Alloa Academy, Clackmannanshire
Bathgate Academy, West Lothian
Baldragon Academy, Dundee
Bishopbriggs High School, East Dunbartonshire
Buckie High School, Moray
Cardinal Newman High School, North Lanarkshire
Castlehead High School, Renfrewshire
Cleveden Secondary School, Glasgow
Dalkeith High School, Midlothian
Duncanrig Secondary School, South Lanarkshire
Dyce Academy, Aberdeen City
Eastbank Academy, Glasgow
Fortrose Academy, Highland
Girvan Academy, South Ayrshire
Glenwood High School, Fife
Gourock High School, Inverclyde
Grangemouth High School, Falkirk
Greenock Academy, Inverclyde
Hamilton College, South Lanarkshire
Hamilton Grammar School, South Lanarkshire
Harris Academy, Aberdeenshire
James Hamilton Academy, East Ayrshire
John Ogilvie High School, South Lanarkshire
Jordanhill School, Glasgow

Kirkcaldy High School, Fife
Kinross High School, Fife
Kilmarnock Academy, East Ayrshire
Largs Academy, North Ayrshire
Lochend Community High School, Glasgow
Oban High School, Argyll & Bute
Peterhead Academy, Aberdeenshire
Prestwick Academy, South Ayrshire
St Luke's High School, East Renfrewshire
St Margaret Mary's Secondary School, Glasgow
Shawlands Academy, Glasgow
Springburn Academy, Glasgow
Stewarton Academy, East Ayrshire

Contents

Introduction

To manage their lives successfully, young people need to be equipped with a 'can do' attitude which will enable them to achieve in all areas - personal, work and social. In a rapidly changing world, schools can help to encourage the development of enterprising attitudes that will equip young people to meet future challenges.

Enterprise in Education

. . . is about developing in young people enterprising skills and attitudes, life skills, an understanding of the world of work and the confidence and determination to take their personal career choices forward.

. . . is a way of thinking and learning. It moves on from more didactic methods of learning to applying knowledge to real life issues.

. . . it encourages independence. Young people need to see opportunities, look for the potential to achieve, and understand their role in shaping this process. This is what we seek to promote in every young person through enterprising learning.

Defining Enterprise in Education

'Determined to Succeed' (Scottish Executive 2002) identified the 4 strands of Enterprise in Education as:

- Enterprising skills and attitudes
- Enterprise activities
- Work-related learning
- Career education

1. Enterprising skills and attitudes
    eg. confidence, motivation, determination to achieve and succeed, awareness of others, responsibility, positive attitude, decision making, informed risk taking, creativity, initiative, independence.

    These are developed through using an enterprising approach i.e. **how** learning takes place. It is about the process of learning. This approach will enable enterprise in education to be embedded in the curriculum.

2. Enterprise activities
    The process of being involved in an enterprise activity will encourage the development of enterprising skills and attitudes such as team building, innovation, planning, organising, time management, problem solving, communication, co-operation, negotiation, flexibility as well as other more obvious business skills such as marketing, market research, advertising, production methods, etc

Activities can be focused on a business start up to provide a product or a service, or be more social in nature focusing on fund raising, a campaign, a exhibition, event, leaflet or book design and production.

3. World of work - including entrepreneurial skills, self-employment and vocational skills

   These activities provide a work-related context for skills such as planning, time keeping, organisation, presentation, communication, resourcefulness, initiative, and build on the enterprising approach. It is part of an enterprising approach that pupils participate in the organising, planning, briefing and debriefing of these activities. Therefore in order to develop a more enterprising approach to work-related learning, pupils must take as much ownership of the tasks involved as is possible.

4. Career education

   While systematic career education programmes are a key part of young people's career development, their ability to take charge of their decisions, take ownership of their career planning and show resilience in anticipating and responding to changes in work and learning can be encouraged through career lessons which are delivered with enterprise methods and approaches in mind.

Enterprising Skills and Attitudes

In our society, it is increasingly expected that our young people become confident, responsible, self-motivated and independent learners, demonstrating a 'can-do' attitude, yet effective team players who are willing to actively contribute to their communities. These capacities are reflected in 'A Curriculum for Excellence' (Scottish Executive 2004) as the four purposes of the curriculum which enable young people to become:

- Successful learners
- Confident individuals
- Effective contributors
- Responsible citizens.

Enterprising Schools

This has become one of the major current focuses for education and the role of school personnel in this process is crucial. Teachers are encouraged to nurture this positive attitude to achieve, this determination to succeed by providing opportunities for their students to experience, and not just absorb, the knowledge provided on school life and life beyond the school.

Enterprising Learning and Teaching

Enterprising learning is about teachers being enterprising in the first instance – looking for the opportunities to deliver the curriculum in a relevant and purposeful way that involves students in their learning and encourages them to become independent and lifelong learners.

© Enterprising Careers, University of Strathclyde, 2007

The key issue in this learning approach is that young people understand that there is the potential for them to succeed and that they can, and do, control the shape of their future. When young people understand that they have choices and opportunities, and are supported by education and guidance systems in addition to family and friends, they can move their lives forward. Teachers have a key role to play in providing them with the skills and attitudes to enable them to do so.

Teachers are learners, too, and it is with this in mind that this publication has been compiled. This book has been written in response to demand from schools and teachers across the country and as a follow up to the earlier publication by Enterprising Careers of '*The Enterprising School'*, 2005.

We are not alone in Scotland in seeing the importance of enterprise education. This is a global issue and is being addressed in many countries around the world in an effort to meet the challenges of a rapidly changing world.

'Enterprise education focuses on identifying and developing opportunities, resources and personal talents, in all aspects of young people's lives' - *Dr Peter Ellyard, Commission for the Future.*

Delivery

Enterprising learning is about *how* we deliver the curriculum. The main features of enterprising learning are:

a. Learning takes place in a *real* context

b. Pupils are given *responsibility* for their learning – eg they make decisions and follow them through i.e. involves taking informed risks

c. Pupils assume *roles* and form relationships with others both internally and externally

d. *Reflection* throughout the learning process ensures that the pupils are aware of their learning, and how they will progress in their learning.

Enterprising Skills and Attitudes

Positive attitude	Flexible
Values	Uses initiative
Responsible	Manages change
Confident	Takes informed risk
Self aware	Determined to succeed
Creative	Achieves
Makes decisions	Seeks opportunities
Team player	Ambitious
Aware of others – respect	Resilient
Effective communicator	Persistent
Motivated	Co-operative
Manages self	Reflects on learning
Manages resources	Gathers and analyses information

Table 1

Developing people who 'can do' needs us to . . .

i. ensure that we enable students to participate in the process and take **responsibility** for their own learning. We should allow them to manage the learning by assuming **roles** and making decisions that will involve taking moderate risk and accepting the consequences. They will have to **reflect** on where they are and where they are going and continually be flexible and adaptable. Continual review of their learning will be part of the process – both content and personal aptitudes must be considered.

ii. provide opportunities for links with internal and external partners in every area of our teaching to create a **real context** for our students to make learning more effective. This will give purpose to our teaching and their learning. It will also develop interest and expertise, add diversity, and provide support and resources.

4

The significance of their learning is greatly increased by involvement in **real** life issues in the world beyond school. External partners are a rich resource for our schools. Not only will this approach provide extensive experiential learning and vocationally-related experiences and understanding, but it will provide valuable information on career prospects and opportunities and assist in career development and planning.

Main Types of Enterprise Activity

In delivering enterprise activity, the 4 main categories are widely recognised as being:

- Presentation of Knowledge
- Citizenship / campaign / social
- Event
- Business

Further details of these approaches can be found in *Section 1: Planners*

Impact

By using an enterprising approach we hope to develop capabilities in young people who, now and in their future, are:

- Can-do, positive people
- Independent individuals
- Lifelong learners
- Effective employees, employers or entrepreneurs
- Active, responsible citizens

A Curriculum for Excellence (ACfE)
This document outlines the purposes of education for a 21st Century.

"It is designed to convey knowledge which is considered to be important and to promote the development of values, understanding and capabilities. It is concerned both with what is to be learned and how it is taught. It should enable all of the young people of Scotland to flourish as individuals, reach high levels of achievement, and make valuable contributions to society."

Purposes of the curriculum:

successful learners	confident individuals
<ul><li>enthusiasm and motivation for learning</li><li>determination to reach high standards of achievement</li><li>openness to new thinking and ideas</li><li>use literacy, communication and numeracy skills</li><li>use technology for learning</li><li>think creatively and independently</li><li>learn independently and as part of a group</li><li>make reasoned evaluations</li><li>link and apply different kinds of learning in new situations</li></ul>	<ul><li>self-respect</li><li>a sense of physical, mental and emotional well-being</li><li>secure values and beliefs</li><li>ambition</li><li>relate to others and manage themselves</li><li>pursue a healthy and active lifestyle</li><li>be self-aware</li><li>develop and communicate their own beliefs and view of the world</li><li>live as independently as they can</li><li>assess risk and make informed decisions</li><li>achieve success in different areas of activity.</li></ul>
responsible citizens	**effective contributors**
<ul><li>respect for others</li><li>commitment to participate responsibly in political, economic, social and cultural life</li><li>develop knowledge and understanding of the world and Scotland's place in it</li><li>understand different beliefs and cultures</li><li>make informed choices and decisions</li><li>evaluate environmental, scientific and technological issues</li><li>develop informed, ethical views of complex issues.</li></ul>	<ul><li>an enterprising attitude</li><li>resilience</li><li>self-reliance</li><li>communicate in different ways and in different settings</li><li>work in partnership and in teams</li><li>take the initiative and lead</li><li>apply critical thinking in new contexts</li><li>create and develop</li><li>solve problems.</li></ul>

Table 2

'A Curriculum for Excellence' 2005

The similarities in outcomes with those expected from Enterprise in Education are evident from the table. Enterprising teaching and learning approaches can make a major contribution to delivering the 4 capacities of 'A Curriculum for Excellence', as can be seen on the table which follows . . .

Enterprising Learning and Teaching

Links with ACfE
Putting learning into a real context encourages **responsible citizens**.

Ensuring relevance to the world beyond school and encouraging participation enables pupils to become **effective contributors**.

Parents and Families
- Partners in learning
- Learn with and from pupils
- Share experiences – life/career/work
- Support learning

Communities
- Establish community/school links
- Add value to school
- Address values of local community
- Social responsibility

Businesses
- Development of employee skills
- Add diversity and interest to curriculum
- Links with future customers, employees
- Provide business expertise

Enterprising Learner
- Accepts responsibility
- Works with others
- Learns success through achieving
- Can-do attitude

The Enterprising School

Links with ACfE
Sharing responsibility for learning with pupils and enabling them to review their progress encourages **successful learners**.

Building relationships with others and taking roles in the process enables pupils to become **confident individuals**.

Enterprising Teacher
- Shares responsibility
- Looks for opportunities
- Facilitates learning

Enterprising L/T
Embedding in the curriculum
- Using the enterprising approach helps to deliver the four capacities of ACfE
- Relevance to the world around
- Adds value to the curriculum
- Develops a positive ethos
- Integrates the curriculum

Connecting to ACfE

How to use this book

There are 5 sections included in the book:

1   Planners

This section provides whole school approaches to Enterprise in Education for all ages and stages from 3-18 years.

The templates are designed to be adaptable for a variety of uses.

2   Integrated Project

Within this section are suggestions for cross-cutting themes, although in many cases one subject area will take the lead.

3   Curricular Areas

This section on 'enterprising lessons' has been grouped into the 8 curricular areas as outlined below from '*A Curriculum for Excellence - Building the Curriculum*' (Scottish Executive 2006)

Expressive Arts	Art, Music, Drama
Health & Wellbeing	Home Economics, PE and PSD
Languages	English, Modern Languages
Mathematics	
Religious and Moral Education	
Science	Biology, Chemistry and Physics
Social Studies	Modern Studies, History, Geography and Business Studies
Technologies	Technical, Craft and Design, , ICT

N.B. Do not be limited by the title or the subject specific areas. These will help you to get started.

The list is endless.

4   Toolkits

This section will provide you with invaluable templates to audit, benchmark, evaluate, record and measure the impact that an EiE approach is having within your school and/or classroom. Collecting evidence is imperative for the success and sustainability of this approach and will be collated for use by HMIe, Scottish Executive and Local Authorities.

5   Resources

Finally, we have provided some website addresses and business links, which we hope will enable you to progress by utilising some of the support available to you. We cannot recommend them all personally, but are sure you will find the most appropriate ones for your particular needs – be enterprising!

It is important that as a teacher using this book, you look beyond the obvious – think out of the box – and apply the formats suggested here to your own work – Only you can see the possibilities and add value to what you do!

Good luck with it and have fun – the pupils will!

Section 1

How to use Section 2
Planning a Project

This section provides whole school approaches to Enterprise in Education for all ages and stages from 3-18 years.

The templates are designed to be adaptable for a variety of uses.

Included are ideas on some popular themes which are very easily adaptable to a variety of topics. They provide guidelines on HOW to approach these themes in an enterprising way. Using an enterprising approach to run a project can bring many advantages in addition to those experienced through enterprising lessons:

- reinforcing learning by putting it into a real context
- developing enterprising skills and attitudes
- learning is directly linked to life within and beyond school
- linking secondary and primary schools (campaigns, transition)
- senior and junior pupils working together (citizenship and PSD)
- stimulating links at parents' evenings (maths challenges, science investigations, current processes and skills)
- participation in school routines (subject options, induction, health awareness)

The added value gained through running a project is that many school initiatives can be addressed at the same time.

We have outlined 9 projects which schools have found valuable as they provide solutions to many current school aims under the enterprise umbrella.

1. Community Links - Campaigns (Active Citizenship)
2. Cluster School Links - Primary Induction Event / Resources
3. External Business Links - Health Event
4. Transitions - Exhibition on Subject Choice (Presentation of Knowledge)
5. Social Enterprise - Fund Raising Event
6. Working Together - Business Event
7. Sharing Skills - whole School Event
8. Burns' Event
9. Valentine's Day
10. St Andrew's Day
11. Christmas Event

Further Ideas
Four Main Types of Enterprise Activities

Presentation of Learning

Applying knowledge gained through the curriculum is one of the most effective ways of learning. There are many applications but it is important that there is an identified audience.

Topics: potential for all subjects eg. local area (tourism, history, community relevance), environmental issues (recycling, litter, bullying, health, safety), application of knowledge – maths and science around us, etc

Audience: peers, other year groups, other schools, parents, community, staff, businesses.

- Presentations on a theme – assembly, parents/community meeting, other schools
- Materials - Welcome Pack 'About our School' for P7 pupils
- Newsletters
- Magazines – creation of articles
- Books – poetry, short stories, recipes etc.
- Brochure or leaflet created & distributed to parents/ school staff/ local community.
- Website
- Display of work for parents' evenings
- Film / DVD/ music CD created on a theme of work
- CD ROM created for the library for pupil and staff use
- CD ROM created eg. to replace yearbook with video clips showing interviews of teachers and pupils, music clips etc
- Create revision games for any subject – for class use

Citizenship – active and responsible approach
(Pupils can launch campaign in school and/or local community)

- Environmental
- Anti-bullying
- Anti-litter
- Dental hygiene
- Health
- Healthy Eating
- Encouraging reading
- Recycling
- Local Town/River clean-up
- ECO schools programme
- Show Box Appeal
- Road Safety
- Youth action group – 'Our Voice'

Event
Pupils taking responsibility for planning, organising and managing an event
Organising external visitors to participate in the event takes it to another level.

- Whole school activity – Theme Day eg St Andrew's Day / Challenge / Charity Event, etc
- Health Promotion
- Induction Event for primary schools
- S2 Subject Choice exhibition & presentations for pupils and parents.
- Sports Festival – hosting various 'stations' with activities, local sports persons giving talks
- Thank You afternoon - for parents/helpers who have served throughout the year
- Cooking Competition – pupils create recipe for local businesses to make and sell
- Fund Raising – sponsored walk, etc
- Fashion Show
- Musical Concert / Talent Show
- Organise and run school disco
- Organise school trip
- Christmas Fayre/Craft Fayre
- Talent Show

Business
Setting up and running a business to sell a product or service to a target market

- Product from Art & Design/Technical/Home Economics packaged and sold
- Books eg. Recipe Book put together by English/ Home Economics/ ICT /Art
- Growing plants with instructions (application of knowledge) and selling them
- Yearbook production
- School Magazine/Newsletter
- Mini Enterprise companies
- Buying products from suppliers, repackaging to sell
- Creating own products
- Providing a service – car washing, Valentine mail, Christmas wrapping
- Selling opportunities at parents evenings, Fetes, school show, concerts
- Auction for charity
- Shares in a company
- Business Dynamics
- Young Enterprise
- Achievers International / ECO schemes

Planner for Enterprising Activities

Stage	S1	S2	S3	S4	S5	S6	Other
Business Model/Selling	Christmas Project *Board Game on intro to secondary school *(SEP)*	Charity Fund Raiser *Show Box Appeal *(SEP)*	Mini-Enterprise Company *Card and Wrap Sweet Thoughts Book *(SEP)*	School Fund Raiser *Book Fundraising Ideas *(SEP)*	Achievers' International *Tourism Leaflet *(SEP)*	Redesign school Uniform Project *Year Book *(SEP)*	Mini – projects Make and Sell *Newsletter *(SEP)*
Citizenship Model/ Campaign	Anti-Litter *Campaign *SEP*	Anti-Bullying *Campaign *SEP*	Eco – Schools Project *Anti litter campaign Plant Kits *(SEP)*	Fairtrade Campaign *Shoe box appeal *SEP*	Health Awareness *Health promoting school campaign *SEP*	Local Community Project *Community Memories *SEP*	➤ Pupils Councils ➤ Firework Safety ➤ Road Safety *Year Group Competition *(SEP)*
World of Work Model/Event	P7 Induction Day	"Make it in Scotland" Day	Industrial Awareness Day	Work Experience	Vocational Training Roadshow	Business Dynamics	
Curriculum Model/Display of Knowledge	P7 Welcome Pack *Parents' Evening for primary*	S2 Options *Peer group displays on subjects /careers*	Department Col. *Parents' Evening Info & PowerPoint*	Community Outreach *Community Memories *(SEP)*	Revision Packs/Games *Study Skills* *Board Game *(SEP)*	Peer Support *Year Book *(SEP)*	Poetry Book-English Firework-Science Newsletter-ICT Recipes-HE Tourism Leaflet - Geo/ML "Memories"-HSE Eng/ICT

*Schools Enterprise programme   Up for Enterprise

© Enterprising Careers, University of Strathclyde, 2007.

Campaign Planner

Topic	Anti-Bullying Campaign (substitute title for any other issues such as litter, vandalism, racism, smoking, etc
Group	Class/year group / whole school / cluster schools Excellent approach to link with other groups
Time	Adaptable - select parts if time is limited
Curricular Links	All - everyone can be involved

Brief Description:
Instead of teaching this topic, students are encouraged to run a **real** campaign and therefore to experience and understand the process - very effective learning.
They discuss the issues, put forward solutions and take action.
They take the responsibility for the campaign with the teacher acting as facilitator.

Enterprising It!

1.   How we made learning relevant by putting into *a real context*

By enabling the students to:
*   decide **what** the issues are surrounding the topic
*   choose solutions, make the decisions and implement the ideas
*   select a real audience to **tell**
*   collect the feedback and analyse their success
*   reflect on their learning – topic issues and personal development

It becomes a **real** situation when they take ownership and make the decisions to deliver to a real audience.
The learning is real and they understand that they can affect other people's opinions and change beliefs.

2. How we encouraged students to take *responsibility*
Teacher acts as facilitator – guidance, support and encouragement

Challenge: define the issues. Student discuss their perception of the bullying problem and their points of view are collated.

Gather more information - students carry out a market research survey to seek opinions of others and get a better understanding of the issues – refine the issues.

What can they do to highlight the issues, raise awareness, change behaviour and help stamp out the problem? Students decide on possible solutions to this problem – generate and select from own ideas. eg. information giving; raise profile through marketing; request for participation, involvement and support; petitions/sign up; meet with others to discuss; run activities; provide support and guidance, etc
Students decide on **who** their audience will be e.g. other classes/year groups/schools/families/businesses/community . . .
A group decision is taken on **how** they will communicate the issues and the possible ways to change behaviours and reduce/stop bullying. eg. presentations, assemblies, exhibition, competition, challenge; written material such as leaflets, books, articles for newspaper, magazines, bulletins; events such as cluster sessions, parents evenings, community day event, inter school challenges; make & sell badges, posters, bag tags, CDs, games, etc

Planners

They draw up a plan of action, taking roles and therefore responsibilities with possible informed risks.

Rate own skills - 'About Me' for self awareness of what role to take. (Section 4)

'Team building' sheets to develop skills in working with others.

Choose roles and groups.

Groups discuss what internal and external partnerships should be formed to assist them in achieving the aims of the campaign.

They take action towards achieving their goals, continually reviewing their own progress to achieve maximum effect. Communicate, co-operate and participate!

The campaign is organised and implemented by the students.

They reflect on their own success and their own learning

---

3.   How we involved partners in the learning – building *relationships*

Market research: other students / support staff in school / teachers / community / business opinions on bullying and how to prevent it.

Support: Funding – where will it come from
Resources – who can supply the materials?

Guidance: Cross-curricular themes – working with other departments.

Education: Linking with other schools.

Business: Bullying in the workplace + prevention, customer service teams. Community issues: police, Local MSP, youth groups, health workers, etc

Audience: Other classes or year groups; other schools/primaries; parents and families; community groups; business as above. If running a competition - use the community/business group above to reinforce importance/ relevance of issue.

---

4.   How we *reflected* on its success - assessment

Open discussion on how campaign was received - perceptions

Request feedback from audience – verbal/forms/response/sales (of badges, books, etc)

Assess how group worked together (see About Us worksheet – Section 4)

Assess personal learning – skills and attitudes as well as effective learning and knowledge on topic itself. (see About My Learning worksheet – Section 4)

---

5.   *Review* – how we can progress from here

Take the campaign to another audience – community for example

Choose another topic and approach it in a different way

Assume different roles within the activity – progression in learning

---

**Planning, designing and development worksheets are available in the
'Up for Enterprise' pack.**

Topic	Welcoming primary school pupils into the secondary setting. <ul><li>Preparation of materials (Welcome Pack)</li><li>Running an event (Activity Day or Week)</li></ul>
Group involved	S1 / S3 / S6
Time	1 day to generate Welcome Pack – see Up for Enterprise Pack 5 weeks to prepare for Welcome Day Event
Curricular Links	All Everyone can be involved

Brief Description:

Students are encouraged to run a **real** event for P7 groups and/or. . .
they can prepare a Welcome Pack for a **real** purpose – issuing to all P7s.

The decisions taken will be based upon their own experiences of moving to secondary school and they will produce a resource for younger pupils - very effective learning and understanding of the issues.
They discuss the issues and put forward solutions and take action.
They take the responsibility for the event/product.

Enterprising It!

1. How we made learning relevant by putting into *a real context*

By enabling the students to:
*   decide **what** the priorities are to welcome new pupils
*   choose solutions, make the decisions and implement the ideas
*   select **how** they will communicate with their real audience
*   collect the feedback and analyse their success
*   reflect on their learning – topic issues and personal development

It becomes a **real** situation when they take ownership and make the decisions to deliver to their real audience.
The learning is real and they understand that they can use their own experiences to provide a better product / service.

2. How we encouraged students to take *responsibility*

Teacher acts as facilitator – guidance, support and encouragement

Challenge: define the priorities. Students discuss their perception of coming to secondary school and the issues they encountered - collate their points of view.

Gather more information - students carry out a market research survey to seek opinions of others and get a better understanding of the issues – refine the issues.

What can they do to ensure a warm welcome? Students decide on possible solutions to this problem – generate and select from own ideas eg information giving; raise profile through marketing; discussion groups; run activities, provide support and guidance, etc

Students decide on their audience of P7 pupils and /or parents:
eg. where they will provide their activity/how they will invite them/when it will be carried out

A group decision is taken on **how** they will most effectively welcome the P7 pupils, e.g. presentations, assemblies, exhibition, competition, challenge; written material such as leaflets, books, articles for newspaper, magazines, bulletins; events such as cluster sessions, parents evenings, community day event, inter school challenges; make & sell badges, posters, bag tags, CDs, games, etc

They draw up a plan of action, taking roles and therefore responsibilities with possible informed risks.
Rate own skills - 'About Me' for self awareness of what role to take. (Section 4)
'Team building' sheets to develop skills in working with others. (Section 4)
Choose roles and groups.

Groups discuss what internal and external partnerships should be formed to assist them in achieving their aims.

They take action towards achieving their goals, continually reviewing their own progress to achieve maximum effect. Communicate, co-operate and participate!

The product or service is organised and implemented by the students.

They reflect on their own success and their own learning

---

3. **How we involved partners in the learning – building *relationships***

Market research:	other students / support staff in school / teachers / community / business opinions on 'Moving to a new place of work – induction processes'.
Support:	Funding – where will it come from? Resources – who can supply the materials?
Guidance:	Cross-curricular themes – working with other departments.
Education:	Linking with other schools. Business - induction into the workplace, HR teams.
Community issues:	Local MSP, school support groups, health workers, road safety, etc
Audience:	All P7 and their teachers; parents and families

---

4. **How we *reflected* on its success - assessment**

Open discussion on how P7 enjoyed it - perceptions
Request feedback from audience – verbal/forms/responses to product or event

Assess how group worked together (see About Us worksheets – Section 4)

Assess personal learning – skills and attitudes as well as effective learning and knowledge on topic itself. (see About My Learning worksheet – Section 4)

---

5. ***Review* – how we can progress from here**

Running the event for parents.

Take different roles within the activity – progression in learning

---

**Planning, designing and development worksheets are available in the
'Up for Enterprise' pack. 'Welcome Pack for P7'**

Working Together

Topic	An event to encourage building relationships between year / class groups.
Group	All ages and stages
Time	Adaptable
Curricular Links	All

Brief Description:
An opportunity for classes / year groups to work together and make links with departments and staff, encouraging good working relationships.

Enterprising It!

1.   How we made learning relevant by putting into *a real context*

The challenge is to create 'Department Door Signs' for the school.

Target market is the staff in the school.
It becomes a **real** situation when they take ownership and make the decisions to deliver to a real audience.

Pupils have to design:
Company Name + Design for door sign + presentation for a panel of judges.

The winning team will have the opportunity to produce their signs for use in school at start of new session – they will be displayed in corridors and on doors in the school.

2. How we encouraged students to take *responsibility*

Teacher / senior pupils to act as facilitator – guidance, support and encouragement

Groups are chosen based on specific criteria set by staff.

The groups then have to:
*   agree a company name
*   gather information about departments and staff
*   generate ideas and discuss the options, deciding on best design
*   work together and take responsibility to complete the task
*   assume roles within their groups and set targets for completion
*   decide on **how** they will present their product effectively to the judges

---

3.   How we involved partners in the learning – building *relationships*

Market research:staff in school / teachers / departmental work

Business: talks and advice from company producing door signs / graphic artists / advertising ideas for communicating themes

Audience: Staff in the school
If running a competition - use the community/business group above to reinforce importance/ relevance of issue.

---

4.   How we *reflected* on its success - assessment

Feedback from judging panel
Open discussion on effectiveness of work produced.
Assess how group worked together (see About Us worksheet – Section 4)
Assess personal learning – skills and attitudes as well as effective learning and knowledge on topic itself. (see About My Learning worksheet – Section 4)

---

5.   *Review* – how we can progress from here

Using as an Induction Event with new P7 coming into school to introduce them to the departments and the staff.

Take different roles within the activity – progression in learning.

**Planning, designing and development worksheets are available in the
'Up for Enterprise' pack.**

Sharing Skills Fun Day   Whole School Event

Topic	Whole school activity involving all staff and pupils
Group	All ages and stages
Time	Adaptable
Curricular Links	All

Brief Description:

A one day event where staff and pupils provide a variety of challenges / activities for other pupils in the school to raise achievement, build confidence and enhance learning. The purpose is to involve everyone in enterprise type activities.

Enterprising It!

1. How we made learning relevant by putting into *a real context*

Pupils/ staff are asked to provide challenging activities for the whole school to participate in during a Challenge Day Event. What talents could they offer?

Target market is the whole school.
It becomes a **real** situation when they take ownership and make the decisions to deliver to a real audience.

They have to create / invite guests to:
> Provide a challenge on the day.

Some activities are organised by the staff and pupils themselves, others by invited businesses.

2. How we encouraged students to take *responsibility*

Management committee is selected to oversee all the activities and to organise the day – timetabling, newsletters, advertising, etc

Other groups take charge of their own activity:
> Food challenge
> Fair trade
> Variety of sports challenges
> Cake decorating
> Photography
> Dog handling skills
> Pottery
> Team building skills
> Study skills
> Making and selling
> And others

---

3.   How we involved partners in the learning – building *relationships*

Business: Businesses involved in providing workshops giving advice and guidance

Community: Community groups participate on the day

Audience: All staff and students in the school

---

4.   How we *reflected* on its success - assessment

Feedback from each workshop – participants and providers

Assess personal learning – knowledge, skills and attitudes gained on the day and in preparation

Enjoyment and relationships built – class discussions

Impact – assessment on pupil / staff relations and pupil engagement as a result

---

5.   *Review* – how we can progress from here

Use as an annual event as it was so successful

**Planning, designing and development worksheets are available in the
'Up for Enterprise' pack.**

Topic	Transition stages – about our subject options - making subject choices at S1 or S2 or S4 or S5.
Group	Year group above who have already experienced the learning
Time	Adaptable - select parts if time is limited
Curricular Links	All

Brief Description:

Event to market subjects in the secondary curriculum.

Instead of telling new students about what to expect from their subject selections, older students are encouraged to run a **real** event to provide guidance on subject content and potential use of the knowledge gained. This is based on their own experience and understanding of what they have learned - very effective consolidation of own learning.

They discuss the rationale, put forward options and take action.

They take the responsibility for the event to promote subject guidance.

Enterprising It!

1.   How we made learning relevant by putting into *a real context*

By enabling the students to:

*   decide **what** were the relevant aspects of their learning in each subject (consolidate own learning)
*   decide **how** they will tell their identified real audience (transfer knowledge)
*   implement their ideas – process of planning event
*   collect the feedback and analyse their success
*   reflect on their learning – topic issues and personal development

It becomes a **real** situation when they take ownership of the topic and make the decisions on **how** and **what** they will deliver to a real audience.

Their learning is in a real situation and they understand that they can, using their own experience, develop understanding of others and affect their decisions.

---

2. How we encouraged students to take *responsibility*

Teacher acts as facilitator – guidance, support and encouragement

Challenge: define the aims. Student discuss their involvement in the subjects and prioritise important information – how it was taught, content, expectations, assessments, potential use in careers and possible extra activity options

Gather more information - students carry out a market research survey to seek opinions of others and get a broader understanding – refine the issues.

What can they do to highlight the subject strengths, raise awareness, provide a better understanding? Students decide on possible solutions to this problem – generate and select from own ideas. e.g information giving; raise profile through marketing/external speakers; discussion/interest groups; run activities; provide support and guidance

Students decide on **who** their audience will be eg. appropriate year groups/other schools/families/businesses - careers/community

---

A group decision is taken on **how** they will communicate the issues and the possible ways to provide this information most effectively. e.g. presentations, assemblies, exhibition, subject competition, inter school challenge; written material such as leaflets, books, articles for newspaper, magazines, bulletins; events such as cluster sessions, parents evenings, make & sell badges, posters, bag tags, CDs, games to promote subject

They draw up a plan of action, taking roles and therefore responsibilities with possible informed risks.
Rate own skills - 'About Me' for self awareness of what role to take. (Section 4)
'Team building' sheets to develop skills in working with others. (Section 4)
Choose roles and groups.

Groups discuss which internal and external partnerships should be formed to assist them in achieving the aims of the campaign.

They take action towards achieving their goals, continually reviewing their own progress to achieve maximum effect. Communicate, co-operate and participate!

The event is organised and implemented by the students.

They reflect on their own success and their own learning

---

3. **How we involved partners in the learning – building *relationships***
  Market research: other students / support staff in school / teachers / community/ business careers.
  Support: Funding – where will it come from?
  Resources – who can supply the materials?
  Guidance: Working with specific departments to focus on key messages.
  Education: Linking with other schools.
  Business: Career requirements; HR dept; FE and HE groups
  Community issues: Families
  Audience: appropriate year groups; other schools (more variety in choice/primaries); parents and families; community groups; business as above.

---

4. **How we *reflected* on its success - assessment**
Open discussion on success of event - perceptions of understanding and information gained
Request feedback from audience – verbal forms/responses numbers signing up where option choices are required
Assess how group worked together (see About Us worksheet – Section 4)
Assess personal learning – skills and attitudes as well as effective learning and knowledge on topic itself. (see About My Learning worksheet – Section 4)

---

5. ***Review* – how we can progress from here**
Transitions for another audience/ year group / leaving school options

Careers Event

Take different roles within the activity – progression in learning

---

**Planning, designing and development worksheets are available in the
'Up for Enterprise' pack.**

Topic	Raising awareness on Health issues
Group	Class/year group/whole school/cluster schools Excellent approach to link with other groups
Time	Adaptable - select parts if time is limited
Curricular Links	All Everyone can be involved

Brief Description:
Instead of teaching various aspects of this topic, students are encouraged to run a **real** event and therefore experience and understand the process - very effective learning both in content of topic and in personal development.
They discuss the priorities, put forward ideas and take action.
They take the responsibility for the event with the teacher acting as facilitator.

Enterprising It!

1. How we made learning relevant by putting into *a real context*

By enabling the students to:
*   decide **what** the main issues are surrounding the topic
*   make choices, take decisions and implement the ideas
*   select a real audience to inform
*   collect the feedback and analyse their success
*   reflect on their learning – topic issues and personal development

It becomes a **real** situation when they take ownership and make the decisions to deliver to a real audience. This is the enterprise process which enables them to develop personal life skills
The learning process is a real situation and they understand that they can contribute to the learning and understanding of other people.

2. How we encouraged students to take *responsibility*
Teacher acts as facilitator – guidance, support and encouragement

Challenge: define the issues. Students discuss their perception of health, what it includes and their points of view are collated.

Gather more information - students carry out a market research survey to seek opinions of others and get a better understanding of the issues – refine the issues.

What can they do to highlight the issues, raise awareness, contribute to an understanding of health and perhaps change behaviour where appropriate? Students decide on possible options available – generate own ideas and select. eg Information giving; run an exhibition involving selection of partners in area of health; raise profile through marketing; make a request for participation, involvement and support; generate petitions/sign up; group discussions; run activities; provide support and guidance, etc. Students decide on WHO their audience will be: eg. Other classes/year groups/ schools/families/businesses/community…

A group decision is taken on **how** they will communicate the information and the possible ways to inform, gain an understanding and, if appropriate, gain commitment to change behaviours and live a better life style. eg. Exhibition, Presentations, Assemblies, Competition (fitness), challenges (food tasting, food science experiments, etc); Written material such as leaflets, books, articles for newspaper, magazines, bulletins; Events such as cluster sessions, parents evenings, community day event, inter school challenges; Make & sell badges, posters, bag tags, CDs, games, on the theme

They draw up a plan of action, taking roles and therefore responsibilities with possible informed risks.
Rate own skills - 'About Me' for self awareness of what role to take.
'Team building' sheets to develop skills in working with others.
Choose roles and groups.

Groups discuss what internal and external partnerships should be formed to assist them in achieving the aims of the campaign.

They take action towards achieving their goals, continually reviewing their own progress to achieve maximum effect. Communicate, co-operate and participate!

The exhibition is organised and implemented by the students.

They reflect on their own success and their own learning

---

3.   How we involved partners in the learning – building *relationships*

Market research:	other students / support staff in school / teachers / community/ business opinions how to maintain a healthy life style.
Support:	Funding – where will it come from? Resources – who can supply the materials?
Guidance:	Cross curricular themes – working with other departments.
Education:	Linking with other schools.
Business:	health and safety in the workplace, HR and customer service teams. Community issues: health agencies, police, community groups, youth groups etc
Audience:	other classes or year groups; other schools/primaries; parents and families; community groups; business as above. If running a competition - use the community/business group above to reinforce importance/ relevance of issue.

---

4.   How we *reflected* on its success - assessment
Open discussion on how exhibition was received - perceptions
Request feedback from audience – verbal / forms / response / sales
Assess how group worked together (see 'About Us' worksheet)
Assess personal learning – skills and attitudes as well as effective learning and knowledge on topic itself. (See 'About My Learning' worksheet)

---

5.   *Review* – how we can progress from here
Taking the exhibition to another audience – community for example

Choose another topic (Fitness, Community links) and approach it in a different way

Take different roles within the activity – progression in learning

---

**Planning, designing and development worksheets are available in the
'Up for Enterprise' pack**

Fund Raising Charity/Social Enterprise Event

Topic	Raising funds to support a worthy cause – active citizenship
Group	Class / year group / whole school / cluster schools Excellent approach to link with other groups
Time	Adaptable - select parts if time is limited
Curricular Links	All Everyone can be involved

Brief Description:

To instill in students a sense of social awareness and belief that they can make a difference for others by providing them with the opportunity to raise funds to support a local or national cause.

Students are encouraged to run a **real** event - experiencing and understanding the process - very effective learning both in content of topic and in personal development.

By discussing the issues, they put forward ideas and take action.

They take the responsibility for the event with the teacher acting as facilitator.

Enterprising It!

1. How we made learning relevant by putting into *a real context*

By enabling the students to:
* decide on the issues faced by charities
* choose a charity to support
* select a real audience to support the charity cause
* choose solutions, make decisions and implement the ideas
* collect the feedback and analyse their success
* reflect on their learning – topic issues and personal development

It becomes a **real** situation when they take ownership and make the decisions to deliver a solution to a real audience.

The learning is real and they understand that they can affect other peoples' lives whilst providing information and understanding by involving others in the process.

2. How we encouraged students to take *responsibility*

Teacher acts as facilitator – guidance, support and encouragement

Challenge: define the issues. Student discuss their perception of the needs of charities and their points of view are collated.

Gather more information - students carry out a market research survey to seek opinions of others and get a better understanding of the issues – refine the issues.

What can they do to highlight the issues, raise awareness, gain understanding of how others can help? Students decide on possible options to support charities – generate and select from own ideas e.g raise profile through marketing; request for participation, involvement and support; petitions/ sign up; meet with others to discuss; run activities; provide support and guidance, Information giving, etc. Students decide on **who** their audience will be: e.g. Other classes/ year groups/ schools / families / businesses / community…

A group decision is taken on **how** they will communicate the issues and the possible ways to raise funds and educate others to their needs e.g. presentations, assemblies, exhibition, competition – fun run, challenge – shoe box appeal, inter school challenges; written material such as leaflets, books, articles for newspaper, magazines, bulletins; events such as fayres, dress-down in school day, car boot sales, car wash, pack a bag, art sale, etc at parents evenings, community day event; make (sell?) badges, posters, bag tags, CDs, games, etc

They draw up a plan of action, taking roles and therefore responsibilities with possible informed risks. Rate own skills - 'About Me' for self awareness of what role to take. 'Team building' sheets to develop skills in working with others. Choose roles and groups.

Groups discuss what internal and external partnerships should be formed to assist them in achieving the aims of the fund raising event.

They take action towards achieving their goals, continually reviewing their own progress to achieve maximum effect. Communicate, co-operate and participate!

The event is organised and implemented by the students.

They reflect on their own success and their own learning

---

3. **How we involved partners in the learning – building *relationships***

Market research:	other students /support staff in school / teachers / community / business ideas on how to support the work of charities / which charity to support.
Support:	Funding – where will it come from to get you started? Resources – who can supply the materials?
Guidance:	Cross curricular themes – working with other departments.
Education:	Linking with other schools.
Business:	links with charities, events, customer service teams.
Community issues:	Local MSP, community groups, health workers, etc
Audience:	other classes / year groups; other schools / primaries; parents and families; community groups; business as above. If running a competition - use the community/business group above to support what you are doing – prizes, funding, people, sponsorship.

---

4. **How we *reflected* on its success - assessment**

Open discussion on how many participated / funding - perceptions

Assess how group worked together (see About Us worksheet – Section 4)
Assess personal learning – skills and attitudes as well as effective learning and knowledge on topic itself. (see About My Learning worksheet – Section 4)

---

5. *Review* – **how we can progress from here**

Another charity but different event

Choose another audience to work with and approach it in a different way (raising funds for a school trip)

Take different roles within the activity – progression in learning

---

**Planning, designing and development worksheets are available in the
'Up for Enterprise' pack. 'Shoe Box Appeal'**

Theme Days

Burns' Day
25 January

Valentine's Day
14 February

St Andrew's Day
30 November

Christmas Event
December

Local/School Events

Burns' Day

Curricular Areas	Suggested Activities

Expressive Arts

Art and Design	Portrait of the Bard – competition Alternative packaging for haggis
Music	Design and perform music programme for Burns' Supper
Drama	Write and perform a short play on life of Burns

Health and Wellbeing

PE	Scottish Country Dancing – invent a new dance Sports theme specific Throwing the haggis!
PSD	Family links 'A Man's a Man for a' that' – equality issues, sex education
HE	Design and provide food for a Burns' Supper. Taste of Scotland foods

Languages

English	Poetry Stories from Scottish Literature Dialects/glossary of terms
Gaelic	Use of language in 18th Century / The 'Mod' Simple Gaelic poetry
Modern Languages	Selling Burns abroad for link schools

Planners

Mathematics	Tax and Customs and Excise! 'The Deil's awa..' Weights and Measures Stats on life expectancy / birth rates past and present
RME	Religious observance in the 18th Century Fund raising for specific event

Science

Biology	Roses 'My Love is like a red, red rose...' and other plant life
Chemistry	Analysing whisky Make a perfume (rose or heather) Analysing a haggis Witches Potions – competition!
Environmental	Farming – human effect on nature 'To a Mouse...'
Physics	Astronomy

Social Studies

History	Tam O'Shanter Historical buildings with Burns' connections
Geography	Burns' Trails Differences in housing and landscape Scottish explorers
Modern Studies	Scottish society in 18th Century The Enlightenment
Business Education	Compiling a book of facts Make and sell Burns' souvenirs

Technologies

Craft and Design	Tartan Challenge!
Technical	Make a traditional utensil
ICT	Analysis of language using software Olde Worlde words on internet Planning of Burns' Supper event

St Valentine's Day

Curricular Areas	Suggested Activities

Expressive Arts

Art and Design	Hearts and flowers theme
Music	CD production of love songs– sell for charity Mini school show
Drama	Performance of Romeo and Juliet

Health and Wellbeing

PE	Sporting partnerships – competition
PSD	Relationships and partnerships/caring and consideration/responsibilities
HE	Creating and making heart shaped biscuits Coffee morning for senior citizens

Languages

English	Compile a Love poetry/ famous romantic poets/ booklet Poetry readings to primary pupils
Gaelic	Cards and poems
Modern Languages	Valentine's cards in another language How other countries celebrate Terms of endearment/romantic cities

St. Valentine

Mathematics	Geometry – hearts and other shapes!
RME	Debate on love and marriage

Science

Biology	Reproduction et al! DNA/genes Anatomy of the heart
Chemistry	Love potions Precious metals and stones Chemical symbols design competition
Environmental	Sustainability
Physics	Physics of sound

Social Studies

History	Famous partners in history Kings and Queens
Geography	Romantic places of interest
Modern Studies	Debate on commercialism
Business Education	Service – delivery of cards/ gifts

Technologies

Craft and Design	Designing a gift from the heart
Technical	Wooden heart with inscriptions
ICT	Designing a message board for pupils to give and receive messages

St Andrew's Day

Curricular Areas	Suggested Activities

Expressive Arts

Art and Design	Design a Tartan Kiltmakers
Music	Scottish song and dance event History of Scottish music New Scottish Anthem competition
Drama	Scottish Play – written and performed Famous Scottish comics – performance

Health and Wellbeing

PE	Sport in Scotland/Scottish Sporting Heroes Shinty / Golf / etc Tournament Scottish Dancing – Ceilidh Develop a modern ceilidh dance
PSD	Our Scottish Citizenship
HE	Scottish Food Fayre Making tartan souvenirs for sale Charity dinner

Languages

English	Debate: Here's Tae Us – Wha's Like Us? Scottish literature past and present Famous authors Discursive essays or poetry book Research history of St Andrew
Gaelic	Introduction to the language involving local native speakers - for parents too.
Modern Languages	Tourist leaflet (The Auld Alliance) Link with partner school abroad Compare National Festivals

Mathematics	Design and create packaging for make and sell Stats of Scotland theme – Profiling Scots Budgeting for a ceilidh Scale drawings for a Scottish building
RME	Charity dinner/ event for pupils and staff

Science
Famous inventors and scientists

Biology	Scottish plants and wildlife information book
Chemistry	Whisky – distillation process
Environmental	ECO topics – eg pollution, recycling, improving environment
Physics	The physics of bagpipes Scottish Inventors Acoustics

Social Studies

History	The Auld Alliance Finding out about our Patron Saint
Geography	Maps/Regions/ Special features relevant to our country
Modern Studies	Debate on Scottish issues Campaign for a Scottish holiday Our Scottish Parliamentary System
Business Education	Promoting Scotland abroad Scottish entrepreneurs Newsletter / programme

Technologies

Craft and Design	Buildings – Scottish Parliament Design an item to commemorate St Andrew's Day
Technical	Scottish Engineering Heritage Make a chanter – competition Create a mock Black House
ICT	Website on our local area/historical facts Posters, tickets, advertising for a ceilidh/event

Christmas Event

Curricular Areas	Suggested Activities

Expressive Arts

Art and Design	Card competition – local business sponsors
Music	CD compilation for selling Carol concert
Drama	Christmas play of own choice/design

Health and Wellbeing

PE	Social dancing Design a new dance for Christmas
PSD	Fund raising events for charity at Christmas – homelessness (Shelter) / Elderly in Community parcels
HE	Make and Bake sale Guess the weight of cake Design a new Christmas cookie Charity Raffle

Languages

English	Dickens – reading to younger pupils, performing Short story competition on a Christmas theme
Gaelic	Christmas cards/carols/choir
Modern Languages	Christmas carols and choir Variety of cards Greetings in other languages Customs in other countries at Christmas

Mathematics	Weights and measures – links with Home Economics Co-ordinates used to design Xmas tags
RME	About giving . . . Christianity Shoe Box appeal . . . eg Salvation Army Other religious festivals

Science

Biology	How to grow traditional Christmas plants and flower arrangements
Chemistry	Christmas fragrances and compositions
Environmental	Sustainable cards/ real Christmas trees/ recycling projects
Physics	Electric circuits – tree lights/ solar lights/ candles Safety

Social Studies

History	Timelines BC / AD The changing face of Santa eg Coca Cola marketing (green to red)
Geography	Middle East past and present Current affairs
Modern Studies	How Christmas is celebrated in Europe and beyond Debate: 'Are we losing the true meaning of Christmas?'
Business Education	Commissioning cards/ gift boxes/ calendars for business use

Technologies

Craft and Design	Design a Christmas gift – tree light/table centre
Technical	Make gifts designed above for sale
ICT	Christmas Carol booklet designed and produced Presentation for assembly on Christmas theme Christmas games

Section 2

Presentation of Knowledge

Citizenship

Event

Business

How to use Section 2
Integrated Projects

Within this section are suggestions for cross-cutting themes, whole school or whole year groups to use although in many cases one subject area will take the lead.
For ease of use we have categorised them into:

4 Main Types of Enterprise Activity

Presentation of Knowledge	**Citizenship**
Business Links in Action	Community Event
Calendar Production	Improving the Environment
Primary – Secondary Liaison	Creativity in the Environment
Work Experience Newsletter	Shoebox Appeal
Creating a Media Network	Assembly Presentations (on Citizenship themes)
Conservation	French play about our environment
	Primary – Secondary Liaison
	Welcome Pack for Induction
Event	**Business**
Health Fair Induction Event	Book – Design and Production
Welcome Pack for Induction	Making & Selling
Maths-fest! for Induction	Designing Product for local retailer
Designing a Phone Cover	Promoting Healthy Eating
Christmas Design Challenge	Theme Day/Magazine
Primary – Secondary Liaison	Yearbook Production
Marketing the School Show	Mini Enterprise

Presentation of Knowledge

Business Links in Action

Calendar Production

Primary – Secondary Liaison

Work Experience Newsletter

Creating a Media Network

Conservation

Brief description
As part of our Career Education Programme, S2 students spent a day working alongside a variety of local employers on 'real life' activities in order to create a business flyer for a company.

"Enterprising" it!

1. **How we made learning *relevant* by putting into a *real context***
   We made this relevant by setting the task of preparing a new business flyer for our associated companies using information they had gleaned on the day spent with the business.

   Students were provided with a basic design brief and were assigned to prepare a draft within a given period of time.

   The 'winning' flyer was then used as a template for the commercially produced product.

   The winning design had the opportunity (with Art Department) to assist the graphic designers and printers who had the contract for producing the flyer on a commercial basis.

2. **How we encouraged pupils to take *responsibility***
   Pupils were encouraged to take ownership and responsibility for this project:
   - by gathering relevant information during their business visits
   - by discussing key messages with businesses focusing on their needs
   - through class discussions with relevant departments
   - by creating ideas to include in flyer and agree format of flyer
   - presenting their final product to businesses

3. **How we involved partners in learning – building *relationships***

External = Pupils made contact with the following:

- Local employers and the manager of the local business community link scheme. These people talked directly to the students about their career backgrounds and the work done by their companies.

Internal = other adults in school.

- The students saw inter-department collaboration which brought home to them the importance of transferable skills and the relevance of subjects to one another. Links were with Art, Business Studies, ICT, Craft & Design and Technology.
- Students also had the opportunity to 'learn from older students' and discuss the relevance of these subjects within the world of work.

4. **How we *reflected* on its success – assessment**

Assessment was carried out by the employers. Not only were they asked to choose the winning design, but they were also required to award points to all those who took part, based on their

- Enthusiasm
- Ability to work as part of a team
- Ability to work independently
- Collaborative skills
- Communication skills.

All pupils responded positively and enthusiastically to the tasks presented.

Pupils reflected on their own learning and achievements – what skills had they leaned, how had they developed personally.

5. ***Review* – further ideas for development**

- This is now an annual event. Each year we look for a different task for pupils to complete.
- In the coming year a link will be made within a unit of work in Home Economics. Junior and senior pupils would work together to plan and prepare a buffet lunch for staff which would involve the school's associated business links.

Calendar Production

Brief description

To encourage cross sectoral work and apply knowledge gained in various subjects and put into a real life situation, a calendar was produced for sale at Christmas involving Home Economics, Business Studies and Art.

"Enterprising" it!

1. **How we made learning *relevant* by putting into a *real context***

   We decided to produce a calendar to sell as it incorporated application of knowledge in all 3 subject areas

   Our audience was the local community.

   We decided to donate proceeds to charity (local hospice).

2. **How we encouraged pupils to take *responsibility***

   Pupils discussed ideas and decided how they would proceed to deliver a marketable product

   Pupils worked in groups and assumed roles to enable them to produce the calendar

   - Home Economics – specific theme, formatting recipes, compilation.
   - Art – cover design, layout and design of page template, advertising
   - Business Education – business plan, management, finances, marketing.

   Pupils were responsible for:

   - producing all aspects of the calendar
   - ensuring that deadlines were met
   - selling calendars to parents/staff and peers at school events
   - deciding on recipient of proceeds

3. How we involved partners in learning – building *relationships*

External = Pupils made contact with the following:
- Business – local printer to discuss best approach
- Business – customer service advice
- Business – marketing advice
- Customers - ie. parents and members of local community.

Internal = other adults in school.
- Asking staff to donate favourite recipes for calendar.
- Working with three departments to produce it ie. Home Economics, ICT, Business Management.
- Working with office staff to compile and promote.

4. How we *reflected* on its success – assessment

- Product was good - £400.00 raised for charity!

- We developed our ICT skills - produced a calendar on Excel.

- We learned how to gather, select, edit, collate and categorise information

- We learned how to work together, co-operating and negotiating

- We learned how to stick to deadlines – time management

- We learned about ourselves – and recorded our personal learning from this experience.

5. *Review* – further ideas for development
- Involve other departments (English – favourite books).

- Run a competition – winners' work will feature in the calendar.

Primary – Secondary Liaison

Producing Language Resources

Brief description
We produced high quality resources in French and German to be used in our primary schools. This took three weeks towards the end of term 3

"Enterprising" it!

1. **How we made learning *relevant* by putting into a *real context***
   Audience: All P6 + P7 pupils and their teachers in our six associated primary schools.
   Actions: Over a 3 week period, we produced a set of resources in French and German to be used by primary schools. All S2 classes chose a topic in either French or German eg. pets. Working in 6 groups within each class they produced a pack which included "Learning Intention Posters", flashcards, board games, boxes and worksheets.
   Relevance: Experiencing planning, resource management, team-building and time-management.

2. **How we encouraged pupils to take *responsibility***
   We generated ideas by formulating a questionnaire to determine the needs of the Primary Schools and started the project with a 50 minute planning session.

   The pupils made decisions and took ownership by dividing up the tasks such as research, format, typing and design, then choosing roles and remits within their groups. Ownership was established by pupils themselves deciding on ideas for board games, worksheets and resource boxes.

   The pupils co-operated through regular meetings to ensure effective communication.

   Initially the roles were chosen after lengthy independent discussions and from time to time the groups decided to change the designated roles as the project progressed and the strengths of the group became apparent. Open communication and regular debriefing sessions took place, which ensured the smooth running of the groups and the completion of the project on time.

3. **How we involved partners in learning – building *relationships***
    External = Pupils made contact with the following:
    - The staff and pupils in the associated primary schools via a questionnaire in the previous term to establish their needs
    - The primary school staff attended a presentation to view the resources at the end of the project
    - The local media was invited to write an article and take photographs for the local paper.

    Internal = Other adults in school
    - All pupils in S2 worked with all teachers in the Modern Languages Department over a 3 weeks period
    - The pupils were in regular contact with the staff in the ICT suite who advised them on layout
    - The pupils had to explain clearly their reprographic needs to the office staff.
    - They had to explain the whole process to regular visitors from the school's Management Team
    - The school's Enterprise Development Officer and the Pupil Support Team.

4. **How we *reflected* on its success – assessment**
    - The final session of the project involved a 50 minute individual and group evaluation session.
    - From 200+ evaluations, less then 10 pupils made any sort of negative comment; all pupils stated that they had thoroughly enjoyed and learned from the experience.
    - Pupils who had made exceptional efforts were given Positive Referral Certificates from class teachers.
    - There may be the possibility of an Enterprise Award at our Annual Award Ceremony.
    - Success is shown by the fact that we are going to do it all again next year.

5. ***Review* – further ideas for development**
    From the evaluations we realised that there was a need for guidance in both planning a project and working in a team.
    We will repeat the project next year but expand on it in the following ways:
    - The Business Management Department will help put together a feedback and additional needs questionnaire in December.
    - Business Management Dept will do advertising for the project before the project starts and run planning and team building sessions with the S2
    - We may consider selling the resources.

Work Experience Newsletter

Brief description
Following our annual Work Experience week, a 'Work Experience Newsletter' was produced by pupils. This was a collaborative cross-curricular project led by pupils and assisted by Business Education, English and Guidance staff.

"Enterprising" it!

1. **How we made learning *relevant* by putting into a *real context***
   Audience: S4 pupils/ employers/ parents/ staff.

   Action: The aim of this newsletter was to highlight the achievements of our pupils and to build links with local firms / employers and the local community.

   Relevance: Experiencing the work-related environment, developing transferable skills and seeing how curricular areas articulate with the world of work.
   This is a whole school cross-curricular project led by S4 pupils involving several departments – English, Business Management and Guidance.

   Following our Work Experience week, a group of pupils suggested that a Work Experience Newsletter be produced to document their experiences whilst on placement

---

2. **How we encouraged pupils to take *responsibility***

   Pupils took ownership and created a small editorial team.
   Pupils requested submissions from **all** pupils involved in the work experience initiative.
   The editorial team discussed and decided which reports to use.
   Pupils negotiated and decided on roles with the editorial team.
   Pupils co-operated with each other by carrying out tasks, assuming roles independently and also as part of the editorial team.
   They decided on articles and layout of the newsletter which incorporated photographs of pupils reports, and employers' comments.

   Pupils also discussed the target audience and to whom it should be sent.

---

3. **How we involved partners in learning – building *relationships***

   External = Business/Community/Parents & Families

   - Local businesses supporting pupils through work experience
   - Employers' Reports were incorporated into the newsletter.
   - Newsletter sent to all employers and local community who offered placements to pupils to raise the profile of work experience and encourage more firms/employers to offer placements
   - Parents also received a copy.

   Internal = Other adults in school

   - School Board/ Former Pupils Association – newsletter circulated
   - Staff – whole school approach to work experience – over 45 members of staff visited our pupils whilst on placement, fostering links with local employers and enhancing relationships between staff and pupils.

4. **How we *reflected* on its success – assessment**

   Assessment in PSE as part of SQA learning outcomes four unit award.

   Self Assessment focused on:

   - Skills/qualities I have developed
   - What I have learned about myself
   - What I enjoyed
   - What I did when I needed help
   - How I interacted with others
   - How I communicated with others.

   Editorial Team looked at:

   - How they negotiated tasks
   - How they worked as a team
   - How they all take responsibility
   - How effective their time management skills were.

   The Newsletter was very well received by all stakeholders. It raised awareness of the work experience initiative and helped our pupils develop further in terms of the four key capacities underpinning 'Curriculum for Excellence' as well as developing 'enterprising attitudes'.

5. ***Review* – further ideas for development**

   - S4 pupils to deliver talks to S3 pupils' "preparation for work experience"
   - work experience DVD incorporating pre-placement interviews/on placement footage/ interviews with employers/post placement views of pupils
   - S4 pupilsto present to Community Forums on benefits of work experience
   - Enhanced links with local businesses in our community
   - Website development - work experience newsletter/photographs.

Creating a Media Network

Brief description

A local publisher works with three formerly separate groups (magazine, enterprise, multi-media) to form a larger group which is responsible for a range of school publications.

"Enterprising" it!

1. **How we made learning *relevant* by putting into a *real context***

    The work produced resulted in the creation of the school magazine, newsletters to parents, a community web-site, podcasting, and a calendar featuring the work of the pupils in the Art Department. The magazine and website are high-quality publications with a community audience – pupils, families and local employers.

    They outline the work of the school and provide an insight into the range of activities which take place. They also serve to showcase the work and achievements of pupils in both primary and secondary classes and across all subjects.

    Since the magazine and the calendar are printed by a local company, pupils have to work to the deadlines and standards as in the world of commerce.

---

2. **How we encouraged pupils to take *responsibility***

    The staff are there as instructors (for example in using multi-media technology), facilitators and advisors.

    The pupils have sole responsibility for:
    *   agreeing roles and responsibilities
    *   ensuring skills are updated
    *   delegating tasks and working to schedule
    *   researching articles and materials
    *   deciding on content and presentation
    *   working within agreed parameters and to agreed standards
    *   seeking advertising support
    *   pricing, marketing and selling the magazine and calendar.

---

3. **How we involved partners in learning – building *relationships***

   External = Pupils made contact with the following:
   - Pupils negotiate directly with the printing company and with potential advertisers
   - Business input in the form of visits to premises (Glasgow Herald, Radio Clyde)
   - Links have been established with the press (Glasgow Herald, Daily Record, West End Mail), local radio (Radio Clyde), and podcast developers
   - Members of the wider community are involved, particularly in relation to the community website.

   Internal = other adults in school
   - This is a cross-curricular project involving staff from 3 subject departments (Business Education, English, Computing)
   - School library
   - Administration staff
   - Pupils in the group liaise with a number of staff

4. **How we *reflected* on its success – assessment**
   Pupils
   - How this process has impacted on their learning of subject content
   - Added value ie development of personal skills and attitudes.
   Staff
   - Impact on Learning and Teaching
   - Effectiveness of enterprising approach to subjects
   - Changes needed to improve process.
   Community
   - Success of establishing school/community links

5. ***Review* – further ideas for development**
   - The community website could host information from community groups who do not have their own websites
   - Podcasting could be developed in conjunction with subject departments to offer an alternative form of lesson planning, revision notes and supplementary material.

Brief description
This project was designed to teach the topic of conservation in an interesting, relevant and enterprising way as part of Standard Grade Science.

"Enterprising" it!

1. How we made learning *relevant* by putting into a *real context*

- Pupils chose their "conservation" topic by completing a research project on an endangered animal of their choice
- This research involved the Internet, library books and other resources
- On completion of the projects, pupils produced an information poster or booklet
- They spoke to the class about "their animal". The talks were filmed
- The class then voted on which animal they would like to 'adopt' and so help to protect
- The class decided how to fund this adoption. They organised a sponsored silence as a fund-raising activity
- A visiting science group – Animates – came to the school and led an interactive session. This involved live animals and the display of artefacts made from similar animals. There were also activities to raise awareness of conservation issues.

2. How we encouraged pupils to take *responsibility*
Pupils took the initiative in this project and:

- chose an animal to sponsor through discussions and their presentations
- decided which form of sponsored activity they would undertake
- took responsibility for planning, organising and running the activity
- participated in the evaluation of the project
- kept the project alive by having colourful displays in the Science rooms and in the corridors
- providing quarterly updates about the sponsored animals by presenting to the whole school at assemblies and via the website.

3. **How we involved partners in learning – building** *relationships*
    External = Pupils made contact with the following:
    Animal charities – via websites, to decide which sponsorship they would undertake. One class decided to "sponsor" an acre of rainforest as well as an orang-utan. Another class decided to sponsor one animal for two years rather than one, since that would be the time they would spend studying Standard Grade Science.

    The Animates visit was an excellent opportunity to meet external experts. The pupils were very enthusiastic about this.

    Some pupils spoke to representatives from the local council and to Scottish Executive Enterprise Department who were interested in the enterprising nature of this project.

    Internal = other adults in school.
    Pupils liaised with the school librarian in the initial stages of the project. They spoke to the school newspaper team together with the English Department and had a report published in the newsletter to parents.

    The ICT Department worked with pupils to feature the project on the school website.

4. **How we *reflected* on its success – assessment**
    - Pupils were encouraged to reflect on what they were learning and achieving throughout the project in relation to conservation
    - Peer assessment was used during the written and filming aspects of the projects
    - Pupils assessed their own personal development through this activity
    - Teachers assessed the impact of this approach to learning

5. ***Review*** **– further ideas for development**
    The project was extremely successful and will be repeated.

    Further developments could be: a trip to Edinburgh Zoo; use of audio-visual resources; speakers from animal charities; use of ICT in project ie PowerPoint rather than posters, extending links with other departments.

    Careers in conservation: researching the work of the Gerald Durrell Trust.

Community Event

Improving the Environment

Creativity in the Environment

Shoebox Appeal

Assembly Presentations (on Citizenship Themes)

French play about our Environment

Primary – Secondary Liaison

Welcome Pack for Induction

Integrated Projects

Community Event - School Liaison

This project has received an 'Active Citizenship' Award in recognition of its innovative approach to pupil-led learning.

Brief description
We organised an event in the secondary school for pupils with special needs to allow them to experience life in a mainstream school.

"Enterprising" it!

1.   **How we made learning *relevant* by putting into a *real context***

   Audience: Pupils from a Special Needs secondary school.

   Action: Organised a 'fact finding' visit to the Special Needs School.
   Organised an activity morning visit to the mainstream secondary by the Special Needs pupils.

   Relevance: Encouraged mainstream pupils from Social & Vocational Skills (SVS) class to consider and cater for the needs of Special Needs pupils within the local community and to work with them.

---

2.   **How we encouraged pupils to take *responsibility***

   - Set the scene – pupils were set the task and discussed possible approaches
   - Generation of ideas – pupils worked in groups to generate ideas under sub-headings eg. fundraising; transport; catering; activities
   - Pupils selected roles within the process eg. fundraising co-ordinator; activity co-ordinator
   - Pupils made decisions about how to raise money to fund the event and organise the fundraising
   - Pupils 'checked-in' regularly with the teacher to give progress reports/obtain guidance
   - Pupils organised and took responsibility for all aspects of this process
   - All pupils in the class had a role.

---

3. **How we involved partners in learning – building *relationships***

External = Pupils made contact with the following:

- Staff from Special Needs school – gave initial permission for project; background information on pupils
- Media – invited to publicise the event
- Local authority contacted to publicise the event, recognised as an example of good practice
- Permission for visits from parents – letters.

Internal = other adults in school

- Class teachers – to obtain permission to be absent from class on day of visit/event
- Janitor/canteen – to arrange for hall to be set-up. Lunch
- Art/Music/Drama/HE/PE – permission to visit departments and sample lessons during tour
- Headteacher – permission to run the event/request to speak to visitors
- School office – information in bulletin/tannoy/newsletter/local press.

4. **How we *reflected* on its success – assessment**

Assessment in this project was mostly formative in nature focusing on self and peer assessment with the teacher acting as facilitator to elicit reflective responses.

Self-assessment focused on:-

- What went well?
- What went badly?
- How can I improve next time?
- What have I learned?

Peer/group assessment focused on:-

- What was successful as a group?
- What was less successful as a group?
- How could we improve?
- What have we learned?

5. ***Review* – further ideas for development**

- Extend the event for more pupils
- Extend the range of activities on offer
- Organise future events with the two groups of pupils.

Improving the Environment

Brief description
The students, as part of a community project, have transformed an unsightly and dirty primary playground shelter into an area where younger children feel welcome and safe.

"Enterprising" it!

1. **How we made learning _relevant_ by putting into a _real context_**
   - Pupils made contact with the adjacent primary school to offer their services
   - They held a series of meetings with the Headteacher and Pupil Council to gather information, hear what the school needed and develop a design brief
   - They made draft proposals and presented them to the Headteacher and pupils
   - Project management was outlined setting a timescale and deadline for the completion of the work.

2. **How we encouraged pupils to take _responsibility_**
   - Pupils had responsibility for carrying out the project themselves
   - Pupils had to work collaboratively to complete the task as well as individually on specific jobs
   - Pupils took responsibility for identifying and costing materials for the project
   - Pupils took part in purchasing and selecting appropriate materials
   - Pupils wrote to the Parent Teacher Association (PTA) of the associated primary school to seek support in funding the project
   - Pupils organised an official opening which included writing to local dignitaries, School Board and PTA
   - They prepared their own press release for the event.

Integrated Projects

3. **How we involved partners in learning – building *relationships***

External = Pupils made contact with the following:

- Pupils made contact with staff in the local hardware store to purchase supplies
- They met with a painter and decorator to seek advice about choosing materials and how they should be applied
- Pupils met with the Headteacher, staff and pupils of the primary school both formally and informally
- Vocational courses in local college of Further Education: Visitors from local College of Further Education talked about careers and vocational courses available.

Internal = other adults in school.

- Classroom assistants and pupil support staff worked with the pupils in the planning and delivery of the project.

4. **How we *reflected* on its success – assessment**

- The project team evaluated the success of the project by interviewing primary school pupils about how they felt about their new playground feature. This was filmed, having obtained appropriate consent from parents. 'Before and After' pictures of the project will be displayed in both schools
- The film will be shown at future Parents' Evenings
- PowerPoint presentation will also be used to inform the local community about project
- Pupils assessed their own learning – skills gained – through this project.

5. ***Review* – further ideas for development**

Each new group is charged with managing its own project. However it will be used as a model of good practice for future years.

Creativity in the Environment

Brief description

The purpose was to allow pupils to have ownership of the school garden.

To encourage creativity and original thinking through:
- **Designing and planting a 'ceramic planter'. The group was given two planters – one to be placed in the school garden and one to be sold**
- **Designing and developing a wall with recycled bottles to enclose the compost heap in the school garden.**

"Enterprising" it!

---

1. **How we made learning *relevant* by putting into a *real context***
   S1 pupils worked in groups with a facilitator to complete an 'enterprise challenge'. Groups worked on the following teams:

   The Planters
   - Ensure that all the plants were arranged and planted correctly.

   The Designers
   - Design a ceramic motif for the pots using ceramic pieces.

   The Marketing Group
   - Cost the items and decide on what to charge for each pot
   - Decide on their customers
   - Undertake a survey of customers
   - Design advertising materials.

   The Builders
   - Work with a facilitator and build a wall using recycled bottles and crates
   - Pupils learned how these same techniques are used by children in Honduras to build community centres.

---

2. How we encouraged pupils to take *responsibility*

- Whole group ideas were generated through the facilitator
- Pupils chose roles - production team, designers, and marketing managers
- Pupils produced the pots and displayed them
- Pupils worked to deadlines to complete tasks
- Pupils costed their products and decided on potential markets
- Pupils recorded their decisions and co-operated to share ideas
- All groups had a rota to sell planters during break time
- The money raised was put back into the garden project to buy more plants.

3. How we involved partners in learning – building *relationships*
External = Pupils made contact with the following:

- Facilitators from local colleges and universities
- An expert in horticulture
- A member of staff who had been to Honduras and had seen walls built using recycled bottles.

Internal = other adults in school

- Classroom assistant
- Retired teacher of Technology
- Art & Design Department
- PSD staff.

4. How we *reflected* on its success – assessment
Pupils wrote about their day in an evaluation sheet – 'About my Learning' (Section 4)
Personal skills were assessed and prizes and certificates were awarded for co-operation and good work.

5. *Review* – further ideas for development

- Other challenges have since been suggested for a future whole day event such as 'The Dream Challenge' – pupils have to write, illustrate and produce a book for Primary 2 children.
- In future, other departments will be encouraged to provide ideas for a challenge
- Investigate the eco-schools project to sustain and develop the idea of the garden
- Set up after school gardening club to encourage parents, grandparents and other members of the community to offer assistance and expertise.

Shoebox Appeal

Brief description
Group to organise a Shoebox Appeal to send to families – Eastern Europe.

"Enterprising" it!

1. **How we made learning *relevant* by putting into a *real context***

   The audience was the whole school – staff, pupils and parents. The group involved was challenged with filling as many shoeboxes as possible with a given selection of items to be sent to adults and children in Eastern Europe.

   Learning was made relevant as awareness was raised and we realised that we could help. We established exactly where the boxes were to go and accessed the Rotary International website which raised awareness of the conditions experienced by the recipients.

   Pupils then investigated ways of raising money to purchase items for the shoeboxes. This involved problem-solving skills to provide a solution.
   They decided to organise a raffle.

2. **How we encouraged pupils to take *responsibility***

   Pupils generated ideas by brainstorming and discussing problem areas such as publicity, finance and raffle prizes.

   "A design a poster" competition was used to choose an advert to market the appeal.
   Individual posters were displayed around the school to advertise the event.
   Pupils co-operated by working in teams to sell tickets.
   They came together as a group to organize the raffle draw.
   They invited the Headteacher and other members of staff to attend.

   Pupils selected roles as designers, sales people, letter writers, purchasers and marketing people through identifying their own strengths and those of others.

3. How we involved partners in learning – building *relationships*

External = Pupils made contact with the following:

- Parents and families were invited to donate items.
- The local media was invited to attend the draw, and the success of the project with the number of shoeboxes filled was reported in the local press.
- Rotary International came to collect filled shoeboxes and spoke to the group, expressing their thanks for excellent contributions.

Internal = other adults in school.

- Every pupil and member of staff within the school was informed by weekly newsletter and by word of mouth to support the project.

4. How we *reflected* on its success – assessment

Pupils were able to reflect on success by recognising amount of money raised – almost £100.00. This enabled them to buy appropriate items locally and fill the shoeboxes. During this time they had to ensure that correct items were put in relevant boxes.

Pupils had planned the activity and on completion they reviewed this original plan.

They identified what they had learned, how they addressed any problems, and identified any changes that were necessary to ensure the future success of the project.

They also considered who had helped them and reflected on how this could have been improved.

The whole project incorporated a very clear broadening of the skills base of pupils The group grew so much in self-confidence and pupils were clearly able to recognise individual strengths and weaknesses. These were identified and recorded on a personal basis.

5. *Review* – further ideas for development

- They will be able to use this knowledge for future challenges and cascade what they have achieved as they approach a similar challenge.
- This could become an annual event in the school.

© Enterprising Careers, University of Strathclyde, 2007.

Assembly Presentations (on Citizenship Themes)

Brief description
Each class was given the task of making a presentation on a selected issue of importance at 'Year Assembly' events.

"Enterprising" it!

1. **How we made learning *relevant* by putting into a *real context***
   The classes were given a choice of topical issues of a national or international nature.
   The purpose was either to inform, raise awareness, convince or call to action.

   In Tutor/Registration groups, they researched the information necessary and made up a presentation to be performed in front of their year group at one of the weekly assemblies.

   Topics discussed were Aids Day, Clean Water, Armistice Day, Holocaust Remembrance, Red Nose Day, African Aid, Drugs Awareness, Smoking Kills.

2. **How we encouraged pupils to take *responsibility***
   - Researched their topic from current information using newspapers, television and web search.
   - Decided upon the nature of the presentation which ranged from single speaker to whole group, each presentation lasting five minutes
   - Displayed posters, presented using PowerPoint, and produced a DVD
   - Pupils were supported in learning about public speaking and presentation techniques.
   - In groups, pupils chose tasks and responsibilities in order to plan, organise and complete the project.

3. **How we involved partners in learning – building *relationships***
    External = Pupils made contact with the following:
    - Charity organisations – e.g. Amnesty International
    - Parent body organisations
    - Local people involved locally with the topic material.

    Internal = other adults in school
    - Pupil Council and Year Group Heads who managed the inserts for school calendar
    - Both teaching and support staff
    - Dining Hall staff for healthy eating and for market research
    - Janitorial and technical staff
    - School Chaplain.

4. **How we *reflected* on its success – assessment**
    Our Assemblies were recorded by senior pupils and media students and this was presented to the whole school through our internal television system and put on our website.

    Peer assessment was used each time for feedback to the presenters and proved to be very successful. This varied in content depending on whether topic was informative/participative.

    Pupils' personal learning was also assessed – confidence and co-operation were enhanced and skills gained were identified for and by each pupil.

5. ***Review* – further ideas for development**
    - Continue to develop this theme as it benefits both audience and presenters. This year we have additional input to the Tutor Groups on the delivery and skills of public speaking in order to develop confidence in our young people.

French Play about our Environment

Brief description

How to be an active citizen in a clean Europe. This whole school initiative links a city clean-up operation and a school litter campaign, educating students about environmental issues in French and working with schools in other countries. The cross-curricular theme links all departments and year groups.

"Enterprising" it!

1. **How we made learning *relevant* by putting into a *real context***
   - Production of a website looking at the environment in a European context
   - Production of an interactive quiz on environmental theme
   - Production of a video diary detailing involvement
   - Production of a play in French – audience was local community
   - Contribution to and selling of a magazine
   - Interviewed by newspapers on the topic
   - Country park regeneration project – community participation
   - School litter campaign linked to city clean-up operation.

---

2. **How we encouraged pupils to take *responsibility***

   S1 took responsibility for regenerating the pond in the nearby country park
   Pupils helped translate the material into French for the play about environmental issues.

   The pupils took responsibility for being active citizens.
   - Pupils produced the play and delivered in various venues to a community audience – they had responsibility for their resources and props
   - S1 responsible for a weekly recycling scheme/communication with teachers
   - S4 developed an anti-litter school campaign.

---

3. **How we involved partners in learning – building *relationships***

External = Pupils made contact with the following:

- Partners in Sweden, France and Cyprus to produce the website
- Community as audience
- Rangers in park as advisors and support team
- British Trust for Conservation Volunteers
- Local Environmental Action Team
- Scottish Parliament.

Internal = other adults in school.

- All departments were involved
- Janitors, Technicians, etc.
- Project co-ordinated by Modern Languages Department.

---

4. **How we *reflected* on its success – assessment**

- Confidence of pupils was very obviously developed
- Motivation to participate in this learning activity was hugely increased
- Increased motivation to learn a language
- Sense of achievement from all was overwhelming
- Working together to produce something worthwhile inspired us all
- Through writing articles for an ECO magazine and being interviewed by newspapers, the pupils were able to reflect on their learning.
- The pupils won 3 prizes for the play, the most prestigious being a European Award for languages, the only Scottish school to do so.
- We are now established as an Eco School through a whole school initiative

---

5. **_Review_ – further ideas for development**

- Scottish Executive approached the school to deliver this 'innovative, international project' to other audiences
- ECO club established to look at improving the school's environment
- Now working towards a Silver Eco Award and hope to gain our Green Flag.

Health Fair Induction Event

Welcome Pack for Induction

'Maths-fest' for Induction

Designing a Phone Cover

Christmas Design Challenge

Primary – Secondary Liaison

Marketing the School Show

Health Fair Induction Event

Brief description
Healthy Living Fair project to encourage primary – secondary liaison, organised entirely by pupils. Developed to foster partnership working as part of Induction process.

"Enterprising" it!

1. **How we made learning *relevant* by putting into a *real context***

   Audience: Pupils from associated primaries and parents.
   S1 pupils and parents.

   Actions: Launch Day with S1 and P7 pupils
   Healthy Living Fair: presentation to pupils and parents.

   Relevance: Experiencing transitions in life and work environments.

---

2. **How we encouraged pupils to take *responsibility***

   Launch Day – pupils from S1 and P7 from all associated primaries worked together to identify what they could produce for the Fair

   Action: For a period of six months, pupils created products with a "health theme". This included artwork, cards, badges, and recipes. Each group took responsibility for their tasks.

   Pupils took ownership of designing and planning for the event and of presenting at it.
   They worked co-operatively and met regularly to plan the event.

Integrated Projects

3. **How we involved partners in learning – building *relationships***
External = Pupils made contact with the following:
- Dental Health Officer, School Nurse, dietician, Social Work Department, Mental Health workers, other NHS professionals, Local Authority Quality Development Officer (Health), and Enterprise Development Officer
- Holistic and Beauty Therapists who worked locally were invited
- Careers Scotland: careers in health profession
- Many external agencies were invited to the launch
- Parents of all P7 and S1 pupils invited to launch
- Local media invited to attend to write an article and take photographs for the local paper.

Internal = other adults in school.
- Art – posters and badge making.
- ICT – photography and presentations, posters, invitations
- PE Department – made an exercise DVD.
- HE – production of a recipe book and a visit from a top chef to design healthy dishes

These were available in school on the day of the Fair.

4. **How we *reflected* on its success – assessment**
- Self assessment – questionnaire
- Feedback from both individuals and groups
- Feedback from parents regarding Fair presentations
- Assessment meetings with Depute Head Teachers, P7 Class Teachers and with the team from schools.

5. ***Review* – further ideas for development**
We have assessed the validity of running another project next year and have concluded that we wish to do it again but in a different format and with a different theme.

We feel that the biggest change should be to give increased ownership to the P7 teachers and to involve other departments more closely within the secondary school.

Welcome Pack for Induction Event

Brief description
We produced a 'Welcome Pack' and organised an event for Induction Week for P7 and their parents to welcome them and raise awareness of the secondary school.

"Enterprising" it!

1. **How we made learning *relevant* by putting into a *real context***

   Audience: P7 associated primaries and their parents

   Action: Welcome Pack production (ideas found in 'Up for Enterprise' Pack, Schools Enterprise programme).
   Pupils selected activities and designed the format of the pack
   Presentations to P7 pupils and to their parents by S1 pupils.
   Devised fun activities as ice breakers.

   Relevance: Experiencing transitions in life and work environments

2. **How we encouraged pupils to take *responsibility***

   Set the scene: PSD classes were set the task and discussed options
   S1 Pupil Council and S6 led discussions and co-ordinated work of classes.
   Generation of ideas and planning – teacher, managers and pupils
   Pupils decided on how their group would move forward – roles and remits (designers, writers, marketing executives, photographers, production teams, presenters, internal communication with other departments, etc)
   Pupils took ownership: created a management group, designed a pack and programme of activities, developed presentations, attended regular feedback sessions with designated senior manager.
   Pupils co-operated: decided on tasks, sourced materials, implemented roles – independently and in groups.

3. **How we involved partners in learning – building *relationships***

   External = Pupils made contact with the following:
   - Parents and families were invited to our information evening
   - Local community links were made to help support project
   - Businesses were contacted to assist with pack sponsorship/provision of resources /local business information
   - Local paper was invited to attend to write article and take photographs
   - Local radio station was contacted: pupils secured a "slot" during Saturday programme.

Internal = other adults in school

- English Department – report writing and writing articles
- Art Department – designing pack, banners, posters
- ICT Department – photography and presentations, advertising leaflets, posters, tickets
- Maths Department – plan of school
- Technical Department – hall design for event.
- Other Departments – articles on expectations and provision for S1 courses.
- Extra curricular courses – managers and participants
- Other adults – janitor, school nurse, canteen staff, librarian, and community police. Photos taken by pupils and published on school intranet.
- School Board / PTA – information and presentations at event

4. **How we *reflected* on its success – assessment**
   Assessment in this case was used in PSE in Personal Learning Plans.

   Self assessment focused on:
   - In this activity I was responsible for………….
   - This helped me learn about……………..
   - I enjoyed …………………………..
   - When I was working in a group I…………………
   - In this project, I decided that………………
   - I had a problem with………………..
   - But I solved it by………………
   - If I was a leader the next time I would………….
   - I liked / did not like this activity because…………………..
   - What I would like to do next time…………………..

   Group Assessment looked at:
   - How did your group made decisions?
   - How did you manage your time?
   - How did you help one another?
   - When there was a problem, how was it solved?
   - Did everyone in the group take responsibility for his/her task?
   - Did everyone in the group make good use of his/her time?

5. ***Review* – further ideas for development**
   S2 course options
   S4 options for Highers
   S5/6 Leavers Event
   Murder Mystery Induction day
   Website development for parents and pupils
   Famous Former Pupils!

Maths-fest for Induction Event

Brief description
The first 'Maths-fest' was held as part of the annual primary 7 induction event.
The success of this Primary/Secondary initiative resulted in this becoming an annual event.

"Enterprising" it!

1. **How we made learning *relevant* by putting into a *real context***
   The annual Maths-fest takes place in the Assembly Hall at High School to which all associated P7 pupils are invited.

   - This involves 24 teams of 4 pupils (2 x P7, 2 x S1) in a day of problem-solving activities.
   - The pupils work together and co-operate with each other.
   - They have to decide which problems to attempt and how to go about solving the problems
   - Prizes are awarded to the winning teams and the event is reported in the local press.
   - P7 pupils gain experience of life in High School which helps prepare them for the transition from Primary to Secondary.

---

2. **How we encouraged pupils to take *responsibility***
   - Senior pupils are responsible for organising the event
   - S6 pupils organise the activities and man the 'stations'. They explain the tasks to the pupils participating
   - They provide assistance when appropriate

---

3. **How we involved partners in learning – building *relationships***
External = Pupils made contact with the following:
- Pupils in our school make contact with those in associated primaries and with teachers from these schools
- Staff from the primaries take charge of the marking and recording and have the opportunity to visit the Maths Department, meet Maths staff and further strengthen links between primary and secondary
- HMIe considered this event to be an example of best practice
- The local paper reports on the event, including a photograph of the prizewinners.

Internal = other adults in school
- All S1 pupils are invited to participate by attempting a qualifying problem
- Janitorial staff set up the hall following an agreed plan
- All members of staff are invited to 'drop in' during non-contact time
- Members of the Senior Leadership Team lend support by visiting the event and presenting prizes.

4. **How we *reflected* on its success – assessment**
After each event, each task used is reflected upon in order to ensure that problems set are appropriate, challenging and achievable.

Feedback from pupils and staff on effective learning strategy has always been extremely positive.

During the event several photographs are taken of pupils engaged in problem-solving activities and these are then displayed in the Maths corridor, adjacent to a board with several lateral thinking problems. This arouses interest in many pupils and motivates them to have a go at solving the problems on display.
The profile of the Maths department is raised through this event.

5. ***Review* – further ideas for development**
- Either before or after the event, a similar event could take place in our associated primaries to ensure that all P7 are engaged in problem-solving activities of this kind. Within the smaller primaries this would take place within 'co-operatives'.
- Additional tasks eg. "Design a Maths poster" on a certain topic, could be included.
- Other subject areas plan a similar activity on an appropriate theme.

Designing a Phone Cover

Brief description
Start up business focusing on a group-led design project

"Enterprising" it!

1. **How we made learning *relevant* by putting into a *real context***
   Audience
   Presentations on results to other S1 Art & Design pupils and business experts

   Action
   Classes were issued a design brief which asked pupils to design a mobile phone based on one of the 'four elements' (Earth, Air, Fire and Water)

   Pupils formed companies to plan, develop and produce mobile phone designs

   Relevance
   Experiencing life and work skills, problem-solving, leadership and team-building skills.

2. **How we encouraged pupils to take *responsibility***
   The pupils had entire responsibility for the development of the designs and for the generation of ideas.

   Pupils decided on roles and remits within their company (managers, designers, writers, marketing, production team, and spokesperson)

   Pupils took ownership of the project; they designed and presented their ideas through relevant feedback sessions.

   Pupils co-operated – decided on tasks and responsibilities independently and in groups.

---

3. **How we involved partners in learning – building *relationships***
   External = Pupils made contact with the following:

   - Business – Pupils sent their designs to existing companies for feedback
   - Internet – Pupils contacted companies via the Internet
   - Pupils researched designs independently using magazines, the Internet, and existing designs.

   Internal = other adults in school.
   - Pupils presented their ideas to staff via pupil presentations
   - Pupils undertook market research with their peers and other staff
   - Other departments: English, Maths, Business Management, ICT.

4. **How we *reflected* on its success – assessment**
   Pupils self assessed and evaluated their own work
   - In this activity I was responsible for . . .
   - During this project I learned about . . .
   - I enjoyed . . .
   - I was challenged by . . .
   - In this project I decided . . .
   - I had a problem with . . .
   - I solved it by . . .
   - If I were a project manager I would . . .
   - I liked/disliked this activity because . . .
   - Next time I would . . .

   Group assessment
   - How were decisions arrived at?
   - How did you help each other effectively?
   - How effectively did the group work together?

5. *Review* – **further ideas for development**
   - Many of the skills and processes have been incorporated in teaching design throughout all year groups
   - Increased use of ICT and focussed middle school project that further develops computer-generated images to allow pupils' work to be presented in a more professional way.

Christmas Design Challenge

Brief description
During a whole day event, pupils work in teams to design a Christmas bauble, produce it, design and make packaging, market and advertise the product.

"Enterprising" it!

1. **How we made learning *relevant* by putting into a *real context***

   Audience: S1 pupils

   Relevance: Pupils were experiencing a real-life production process.

   Action: Pupils were given a design brief by a local business involved in producing packaging.

   Pupils were divided into teams and were required to select a business name, a product name and an advertising strategy before being sent to production; marketing and design challenges.

   The day finished with a Trade Fair where each team displayed their product and sales strategy.

2. **How we encouraged pupils to take *responsibility***

   Set the scene – the challenge was explained to teams.
   S6 pupils took responsibility of assisting in the organisation of the challenge.

   Generation of ideas – pupils made initial decisions re. business name then proceeded to make further key decisions at the start of each stage of the process eg. marketing.

   Pupils chose roles eg. production manager, advertising manager.

   Pupils chose tasks within each part of the process.

   Pupils took ownership of all elements of the process with the only adult intervention taking the form of facilitator (an adult from the local community).

Integrated Projects

3. **How we involved partners in learning – building** *relationships*
External = Pupils made contact with the following:
- Parents and families were invited to the Trade Fair
- The event took place in collaboration with a local business partner
- Local community members acted as facilitators
- Local press were invited to cover the event.

External = other adults in school
- This was a cross-curricular event – Art, Music, Business Education, ICT and Social & Vocational Skills (SVS) Departments all took part
- All staff were invited to visit the challenge to observe
- Senior pupils helped in all aspects of the challenge.

4. **How we** *reflected* **on its success – assessment**
- All S1 pupils who participated were required to evaluate the event in terms of its success ie. What went well? What could be improved?
- Staff were also asked to evaluate the challenge as did business partners and facilitators.
- All pupils assessed their personal learning.

5. *Review* **– further ideas for development**
- Baubles and packaging could actually be produced
- Extend the event into a series of lessons rather than a one-off event.

Brief description
Organised by S1 pupils, groups of P6 pupils from each of our associated primaries designed an advertising poster, ticket and programme cover for our school show.

"Enterprising" it!

1. **How we made learning *relevant* by putting into a *real context***

   This was a very 'real context' because the winning designs would be used to market our school production. These materials promoted our production throughout the local community and were made available on the evenings of performances to members of the public.

   S1 pupils worked with groups of Primary 6 pupils from each of our associated primaries. They developed a strategy and assisted primary pupils in completing task.

2. **How we encouraged pupils to take *responsibility***

   Pupils had to work collaboratively as part of a team to produce a template advertising the school show.

   Pupils selected individual tasks which they were required to complete within a specified period of time. The tasks all contributed to the overall final product.

   S1 pupils were team leaders. They had to motivate, guide and advise on the way forward and monitor the development of the project.

   Each team prepared and presented a submission on their product to the school show production team.

3. **How we involved partners in learning – building *relationships***
   External = Pupils made contact with the following:
   - Primary pupils met with a number of secondary subject specialists, heard informally about the subjects they taught and about their role in the school show. Our school show production team members were also heavily involved throughout the day.

   Internal = other adults in school.
   - School Technicians and Office Staff were involved in assisting with the quality of the final product.
   - Senior pupils distributed posters and sold programmes.

4. **How we *reflected* on its success – assessment**
   - Pupils were asked for informal feedback on the day
   - Challenge team was asked to reflect on whether criteria had been met
   - A follow-up meeting was held to identify strengths and weaknesses of the day and what required to be changed for future
   - Primary schools were asked to review the success of the day with students and then feedback to us
   - All pupils were given an opportunity to reflect on their personal learning.

5. ***Review* – further ideas for development**
   - This was the first attempt at an annual enterprise challenge. It was such a success that we intend to extend the number of teams next year and include more subject Departments. We also hope to link it in with another curriculum project with our associated primaries.

Book – Design and Production

Making & Selling

Designing Product for Local Retailer

Promoting Healthy Eating

Theme Day/Magazine

Yearbook Production

Mini Enterprise

Book – Design and Production

Brief description
We created a cookbook for students with recipes donated by teachers in the school. The easy to use cookbook of healthy, fun recipes was sold at a Parent Teachers Association (PTA) Trade Fair held in the school.

"Enterprising" it!

1. **How we made learning *relevant* by putting into a *real context***
   Senior pupils set up a company to learn about business set-up.
   They met to discuss possible ideas. They wanted to produce a useful product targeted at S6, many of whom would be going onto university and living independently. A cook book seemed the ideal venture to pursue.

   Since ours is a fair trade town, the company felt it fitting to include a selection of Fairtrade food goods. This involved contacting the Fairtrade charity organisation and ordering stock, selling it and sending money back. The pupils were proud to support such a worthwhile charity. They created a kitchen themed stall at the PTA Trade Fair and were delighted to sell out of all products and even receive orders to produce more cookbooks!

2. **How we encouraged pupils to take *responsibility***
   The pupils used timetabled periods to create the book, but also gave up free time (lunchtime/interval and after school) to work on the project.

   Firstly, roles were chosen.
   Recipes were collected from staff members. The group ensured ease of use for students by dividing the book into sections.
   The design team created a sophisticated front cover design. The pages of the book were created using Microsoft Publisher and were bound together to complete the manufacturing process.
   To supplement the cookbook, the team sourced affordable wooden utensils and prepared them for resale: by drilling, sanding, oiling and decorating them with ribbon. The company parcelled three utensils together with each cookbook.
   They were sold at the Trade Fair. Posters were made to advertise this event around the school building.
   The group had to write a business report.
   The group was responsible for preparing a presentation on their business to school groups/linked schools/PTA/School Staff & School Board.

Integrated Projects

3. How we involved partners in learning – building *relationships*
External = Business/Community/Parents & Families

- Young Enterprise Scotland Company (YES) provided two Business Advisers to visit the team to discuss issues and offer support and advice to pupils
- An external business consultant delivered the "School Navigator Course". This module based course allows pupils to gain valuable insight into the world of business and in particular to business start-up.

Internal = Other adults in school

- Links with ICT, Business Studies and Home Economic Departments.

4. How we *reflected* on its success – assessment
Pupils continually discuss achievements at company meetings and at designated times evaluated the company progress

Pupils took part in a voluntary "Strathclyde Business School" exam which allows them to reflect on their time as part of the company.

Pupils reflected on their skills development and their achievements through this experience.

5. *Review* – further ideas for development
- Future liaison with Young Enterprise Scotland (YES) and its business advisers
- Engage with local businesses to link with school and Local Authority Development Plans.

Brief description

Pupils in Business Education and Home Economics worked together and applied their subject knowledge to make and sell products.

Their products were sold at school events.

"Enterprising" it!

1. **How we made learning *relevant* by putting into a *real context***
   The aim was to develop skills in both subject *areas:* ie. product design, manufacturing, quality control, cash flow, profit, organisation and management.

   As a group, pupils researched the target market and chose suitable products to make and sell. They visited retailers and wholesalers as part of their research. The items which were made were sold by the pupils at Parents' Evenings and at school discos.

2. **How we encouraged pupils to take *responsibility***
   The pupils worked in groups assuming roles in
   - creating/ designing and manufacturing sellable products
   - quality control
   - marketing
   - research
   - financial control. Pupils were allocated a budget and their aim was to make the highest profit, whilst maintaining a quality product.

3. How we involved partners in learning – building *relationships*

External = Business/Community/Parents & Families

- Businesses were involved in research on product, sales, quality and customer service
- Parents were involved as stalls were set-up at Parents' Evenings
- Members of the local community were invited to event.

Internal = Other adults in school

Pupils developed cross-curricular links in Home Economics and Business Education, which encouraged and inspired them. Pupils also sold items of their choice at events within the school and, as a result, interacted with parents, staff and other pupils.

4. How we *reflected* on its success – assessment

Pupils reflected on the quality of goods sold, including the packaging and its effectiveness, advertising, marketing and display of products.

They also reflected on their self awareness and awareness of others. They learned a great deal from each other. Successes were acknowledged and celebrated.

They assessed personal skills development in key areas such as decision-making, taking responsibility, working with others, showing initiative, creativity, and problem-solving.

They had a better understanding of the application of both subjects and their learning became more effective.

5. *Review* – further ideas for development

- The links between Home Economics and Business Education were greatly enhanced during this project.
- Since the project was 'real' the subjects became much more relevant to the pupils. Ideally, timetabled classes would assist future developments.

Designing a product for local retailer

Brief description

We designed new packaging for *"The Fry Inn"* – our local fish and chip Shop (as part of our S3 Design Studies Course). The box had to hold a fish supper and reflect the town and its fishing heritage.

"Enterprising" it!

1. **How we made learning *relevant* by putting into a *real context***

   The owner of the chip shop produced the brief and showed us examples of the previous box. He explained that he needed something bright and cheerful to advertise his business and to reflect the town's fishing heritage.

   The winning design would have the winner's name on the box flap so that each time someone has a supper they will see the name!

   We researched the fishing industry on the internet, brainstormed, developed ideas, and evaluated each others' designs before producing the final design.

   Members of staff of '*The Fry Inn*' chose the winning submission.

2. **How we encouraged pupils to take *responsibility***

   Our initial brainstorming session was a whole group exercise – building a mind map on "Fishing and Our Town". Everyone was encouraged to contribute.

   We looked at examples of packaging and made comments on what worked and what didn't. We realised that 'busy' wasn't always best!

   We generated ideas on our own, solving problems as they occurred and checking with our classmates if the design worked ie. had visual impact and could be easily read.

   We had to keep to deadlines as the owner needed to update the printer with new developments. Some of us scanned our artwork and used the fonts to make it look more professional.

3. **How we involved partners in learning – building *relationships***
External = Pupils made contact with the following:

- Business owner kept regular contact at each stage of the process
- The *Local Advertiser* and the *National Press* featured our project and how we tackled it.

Internal = other adults in school.
- Departments included Art & Design, Home Economics, English (links with the local press), ICT & Business Studies.

---

4. **How we *reflected* on its success – assessment**
Reflection in the design project is done at various stages and often throughout – what looks good, what doesn't, do we need more images, should we use the PC to make the lettering better/bigger/a different colour . . . ?

We evaluated with our peers, buddies and the teachers on a continuous basis and then had to make our own decisions about how to progress.
We were continually being assessed by our teacher.
The shop owner had to take our products away earlier than expected!

We assessed our own learning – What were we good at? Where did we need to improve?

---

5. ***Review* – further ideas for development**
We realise that timescales can change when dealing with the real world and we need to think ahead and plan well for our S4 Design Unit. We could approach other chip shops/takeaways to create competition(!) or design packaging for the school canteen.

Promoting Healthy Eating

Brief description

A group of S5/6 pupils formed the "Tutti Frutti" Company to sell fruit and smoothies to pupils and staff to encourage healthy eating.

"Enterprising" it!

1. **How we made learning *relevant* by putting into a *real context***
   Audience –Whole school (staff and pupils)
   Associated primary schools

   Action – Company was set up and finance was sourced for start-up
   Pupils consulted staff and pupils via a questionnaire
   Business start-up was investigated
   Pupils gained a food handling certificate with support from local college and prepared fruit & smoothies to sell at break times
   A system for ordering the product was put in place
   Pupils also supplied fruit to local primary schools.

   Relevance – Experience of setting up and running a small business.

2. **How we encouraged pupils to take *responsibility***
   Ideas were generated about healthy eating and discussion was facilitated by teacher.

   Decision was taken to focus on fruit and smoothies as the products.

   Pupils chose roles, remits were negotiated and agreed. A Company Director was appointed.

   Pupils took ownership by:
   - drafting and designing consultation questionnaire
   - sourcing the supplier of fruit
   - designing posters to market their service and products
   - planning, organising and producing product for sale.

3. **How we involved partners in learning – building *relationships***
   External = Pupils made contact with the following:
   - Community Health project "Kids & Co" supplied fruit
   - College – worked with pupils to achieve a certificate in handling food
   - Community Action Fund – provided start-up costs
   - Works with local supermarket – how and where they source healthy drinks.

   Internal = other adults in school
   - Health Development Officer
   - Learning Community Employability Enterprise Officer
   - School Art & Design & Technology Departments
   - School Nursery Service.

4. **How we *reflected* on its success – assessment**
   The group continually assessed their progress by reviewing their Business Plan and making any changes required to maximise their profit
   - business skills
   - flexibility
   - planning
   - marketing.

   They did this through group self-assessment and market research.

   Assessment of personal learning gained through process re. self-awareness, working with others, etc.

5. ***Review* – further ideas for development**
   - Pupils now involved with local primary schools as peer educators on Healthy Eating. Pupils are planning and delivering lessons on healthy eating.
   - Prince's Scottish Youth Business Trust: business start-up for 18+. Future Link to be established.

Brief description
To organise the collection of Valentine's messages from pupils and to create a magazine of messages to be sold on Valentine's Day to raise funds for a residential activity.

"Enterprising" it!

1. **How we made learning *relevant* by putting into a *real context***
    Our pupils wanted to take part in a residential trip but required funds to ensure the success of the project. This was the reason for the activity.
    *   We brainstormed ideas that would create revenue for a proposed future residential trip.
    *   The group as a whole then voted on their preferred idea – the option that was finally chosen was to create a Valentine magazine which would contain messages from pupils and be sold in the school on Valentine's Day.
    *   Pupils selected their own small working groups and decided on roles and responsibilities such as marketing, sales and pricing, production etc.

    The small groups then reported back and the class as a whole voted on the suggestions.

    The final sales, marketing and pricing strategy was written up.

2. **How we encouraged pupils to take *responsibility***
    The group took full responsibility for the entire decision-making process including selection, voting on choices, working in small groups – then coming together as a whole to report back and vote on major decisions.

    They had to co-operate in order to attain the end result.

    They were responsible for collection of messages, formatting and creating the magazine.

Integrated Projects

3. **How we involved partners in learning – building _relationships_**
    External = Pupils made contact with the following:
    - Community Education - helped with copying and binding the magazine
    - A local craftswoman was also invited up to show the pupils ideas for designing and writing a front cover.

    Internal = other adults in school
    - The Headteacher was approached by pupils asking for permission to hold the sale and to have message collection boxes in designated areas throughout the school
    - Pupils requested support from janitors to set out tables for the day of the sale
    - ICT Department – pupils arranged with them that the group could use equipment to type messages etc.

4. **How we _reflected_ on its success – assessment**
    The pupils created a report stating their achievements individually and as part of a group.

    During group discussions they realised what skills they had developed and how others in the group had helped them.

    They initially focused on what they as individuals were responsible for and had learned.

    They also looked at how the group felt about the voting process and if they felt it was a successful way to make decisions.

5. _Review_ – **further ideas for development**
    - They could have made/sold more and had greater profit as magazines sold out quickly
    - They looked at future projects and how they could use what they learnt
    - They realised that the initial idea had given them confidence to try a bigger enterprise activity
    - They decided to organise a football tournament for S1–S4, which would again help raise funds for a residential visit.

Yearbook Production

Brief description
Senior pupils produced a Yearbook which documented the year for upper school students liaising with a production company and designers

"Enterprising" it!

1. **How we made learning *relevant* by putting into a *real context***
   - The target audience for the Yearbook was fellow S5/6 students, family members and members of staff.
   - A professionally printed book was to be produced as the book would be sold throughout the school
   - Senior students would create, develop the ideas and manage the production and sales reflecting what a normal business would do.

2. **How we encouraged pupils to take *responsibility* by**
   - discussing what items should be included in the Yearbook - and coming to an agreement on content
   - choosing roles such as editors, photographers and fund raisers
   - liaising with Senior Management, other staff and fellow students
   - taking ownership of the task, setting deadlines, meeting with link staff members and motivating each other.
   - attending meetings throughout the year with the various people involved to keep communication flowing at all stages
   - working both collaboratively and independently to ensure the task was completed.

3. **How we involved partners in learning – building *relationships***
    External = Pupils made contact with the following:
    - Publishers to produce and design the Yearbook
    - Parents for permission to take and use pictures
    - Businesses regarding advertising in the Yearbook to assist in raising funds.

    Internal = other adults in school
    - Other members of S5/6 and members of staff were contacted for photos and articles
    - Other pupils to sell advertising space, allowing students to combine their strengths.

4. **How we *reflected* on its success – assessment**
    - Pupils self-evaluated and reflected on their experience, assessing what they had learned about themselves
    - Link teachers discussed what was learned with students and some of the S5 cohort stayed on the team the following year to pass on lessons learned about running a successful business.

5. ***Review* – further ideas for development**
    - To continue with it, making slight alterations by learning from our mistakes
    - Creation of a web version in future for former pupils to keep in touch
    - Creation of a DVD to accompany the Yearbook.

Brief description
Business Management classes set up a mini enterprise to reinforce their learning in Business Education.

"Enterprising" it!

1. **How we made learning *relevant* by putting into a *real context***
   The class had to produce quality products for sale in the school, to parents and the local community. The products were advertised in school on posters and the pupils set up a stall in the foyer at lunchtimes and at Parents' Evenings. This activity reinforced the lessons learned during the S6 Business Management class.
   Pupils also presented at school assemblies and produced articles for local press.

2. **How we encouraged pupils to take *responsibility***
   - The scene was set and ideas generated
   - Through group discussion the pupils decided on their products
   - Ownership was stressed to the pupils: they had to take full responsibility for the production, marketing and selling of the goods. The pupils were also responsible for contacting the supplier when items were missing from the order
   - The pupils worked in production teams and also made rotas for manning their stall at selling events
   - An election was held for the selection of roles within the company. Pupils made nominations and these were seconded. Voting took place for the two main roles of Finance Manager and Managing Director
   - At all times the pupils made all the decisions relevant to the running of their company.

3.   **How we involved partners in learning – building *relationships***
     External = Pupils made contact with the following:

     - Business Manager - local link - came to the school to discuss the project with the company
     - Parents and families and the local community were a major market for the company
     - Selling to city shoppers through participation in Young Enterprise National Event.

     Internal = other adults in school.

     - During the market research stage, the pupils gave a short presentation to year group assemblies. The pupils had to organise and discuss this with the relevant member of senior management.
     - An article was also prepared for the school newsletter.

4.   **How we *reflected* on its success – assessment**
     Pupils were involved in evaluation at many stages of the project eg. when the products were manufactured, during the marketing campaign and when selling. A number of changes were made to the roles of individuals in the light of feedback and to the way some of the products were produced.

     Assessment of personal development was incorporated throughout and skills attained were recorded.

5.   ***Review* – further ideas for development**
     Another type of enterprise experience will be offered to a similar cohort of pupils for S5 Business Management this session. The experience may be moved to S4. However the timescale required and other commitments on pupils at this stage may require more organisation.
     The experience may also be extended to pupils outwith the subject department.

Section 3

How to use Section 3
Curricular Areas

This section on 'enterprising lessons' has been grouped into the 8 curricular areas as outlined in '*A Curriculum for Excellence - Building the Curriculum*' *(Scottish Exec 2006). These are:*

Expressive Arts	Art and Design Music Drama
Health & Wellbeing	Home Economics PE PSD
Languages	English Modern Languages
Mathematics	
Religious and Moral Education	
Science	Biology Chemistry Physics
Social Studies	Modern Studies History Geography Business Studies
Technologies	Technical Craft and Design ICT

Subjects:

Within each subject, ideas are easily transferable.

By changing the lesson 'topic', the format of the lesson can be applied to other areas.

The same topic can be 'enterprised' in different ways

- Look at the Maths section
- Scan through the following table and look for potential lessons for use in **your** classroom
- Look for partners within the school and share ideas with colleagues

Curricular Areas:

Lessons can be easily transferred from one curricular area to another. For example, the 'Creating a Booklet or Leaflet' template in Social Studies is easily transferable to Home Economics, English or Biology.

Themes:

Some themes appear in a number of curricular areas:

- 'Event' theme can be found under Drama, Modern Studies, Languages, RME
- 'Marketing' appears within several subject areas such as Technology, Business Ed, Music
- 'Design' theme is included in Languages, Art & Design, Home Economics and Maths.

Curricular Areas

Curricular Areas

Curricular Area	TOPIC	Expressive Art	Health and Wellbeing	Language	Mathematics	RME	Science	Social Studies	Technologies	PARTNERS / LINKS	AUDIENCE (Business Community Family Peers)	Page No.
EXPRESSIVE ARTS	Exhibition	✓✓	✓	✓					✓✓	Art Gallery Professionals	F P	111
	Showcase of Work	✓✓	✓						✓	Artist in Residence	F	113
	Sustainable Design	✓✓			✓		✓✓	✓	✓✓	Architects Draughtsmen	C P B	115
	CD Production	✓✓	✓	✓				✓✓	✓✓	Music Professionals Graphic Designers	B C	117
	Talent Workshops	✓✓							✓✓	Music Coaches	C P F	119
	Performance and Workshops	✓✓		✓						Music Companies	P F	121
HEALTH AND WELLBEING	Theatre Production	✓✓	✓✓	✓✓					✓✓	Theatre Companies	F C P	123
	Encouraging Participation	✓✓	✓✓						✓✓	Health Professionals	P	127
	Skills Presentation	✓✓	✓✓	✓✓					✓✓	Media Fitness Advisors	P F	129
	World of Work	✓	✓✓	✓✓	✓			✓	✓✓	Hospitality Industry Media	F C	131
	Design and Make Activity	✓	✓✓	✓✓	✓		✓	✓	✓	Nutritionist Chef Food Technologist	B F P	133
	Product Development	✓✓	✓✓						✓✓	Food Industry Media	B	135
	Skills for Work	✓✓	✓✓						✓✓	Further Education Careers Scotland	B F	137
	Road Safety	✓✓	✓✓	✓				✓	✓✓	Police Local Council	P C	139
	School Environment	✓	✓✓	✓				✓	✓✓	Local Authority	P C	141

Curricular Areas

LANGUAGES

TOPIC	Expressive Art	Health and Wellbeing	Language	Mathematics	RME	Science	Social Studies	Technologies	PARTNERS LINKS	AUDIENCE	Page No.
Writing for a Movie	✓✓		✓✓				✓	✓	Film Industry	B F P	145
Public Speaking	✓✓		✓✓		✓		✓	✓	Rotary International	B C	147
Children's Storybook	✓✓		✓✓					✓✓	Graphic Designer Book Retailer	P F C	149
Presentation Skills	✓✓	✓	✓✓					✓	Language Advisors	B F P C	151
Translating for Local Businesses	✓		✓✓				✓	✓	Tourism Industry	B P C	153
Exciting Cities!	✓	✓	✓✓				✓	✓	Travel Agent	P C	155
Catwalk!	✓✓		✓✓				✓	✓	Fashion Industry Media	C P	157
Making a DVD	✓✓		✓✓				✓	✓✓	Language Agencies	C P	159
Twinning Towns	✓✓		✓✓				✓	✓✓	Partner School Tourism	P	161

	TOPIC	Expressive Art	Health and Wellbeing	Language	Mathematics	RME	Science	Social Studies	Technologies	PARTNERS LINKS	AUDIENCE	Page No.
MATHEMATICS	Truffle Factory	✓	✓✓		✓✓				✓✓	Entrepreneur Food Industry	P	165
	Activity Stations	✓✓	✓✓		✓✓		✓✓			CITB	P	167
	Retail Sales				✓✓				✓✓	Marketing and Sales Personnel	P	169
	Number Partners	✓		✓	✓✓				✓✓	Bank Advisers	P F	171
RELIGIOUS AND MORAL EDUCATION	Human and Moral Issues	✓✓	✓			✓			✓✓	Charities Auctioneer	P	175
	Creative Power CD	✓✓				✓			✓✓	Music Professional	P C	177
	Justice in the World	✓				✓			✓	SCIAF World Health Organisation	P	179
	Religious Observance Conference					✓				Religious Advisors Scripture Union Youth Workers	P	181

Curricular Area	TOPIC	Expressive Art	Health and Wellbeing	Language	Mathematics	RME	Science	Social Studies	Technologies	PARTNERS LINKS	AUDIENCE	Page No.
SCIENCE	Sharing Learning		✓✓				✓✓		✓	ECO Schools and Science Advisors	P F	185
SCIENCE	Scientists at Work			✓			✓✓		✓	Marine Biologist Careers Advisor	P F	187
SCIENCE	Business and the Curriculum			✓			✓✓		✓✓	Garden Centre FE College	P C	189
SCIENCE	Third World Support	✓		✓			✓✓		✓✓	SCIAF Fairtrade	P C F	191
SCIENCE	Power Providers	✓		✓	✓		✓✓	✓	✓✓	National Power Companies	P	193
SOCIAL STUDIES	Fairtrade	✓		✓				✓✓	✓	UNICEF Fairtrade	P	197
SOCIAL STUDIES	Weather			✓				✓✓	✓✓	Met Office AA/RAC	P F	199
SOCIAL STUDIES	Party Politics	✓		✓				✓✓	✓	MSP Local Councillors	P	201
SOCIAL STUDIES	Mock Trial	✓		✓✓				✓✓		Cluster Schools Sheriff Court and Linked Services	B F P C	203
SOCIAL STUDIES	New Business Opportunity			✓✓			✓	✓✓	✓✓	Business Forums Local Council	B P C F	205
SOCIAL STUDIES	Entrepreneur of the Future	✓		✓				✓✓	✓✓	YES Bank	B	207
SOCIAL STUDIES	Board Game Bonanza	✓		✓				✓✓	✓✓	Manufacturer	P	209
SOCIAL STUDIES	Business in Action	✓		✓				✓✓	✓	PSYBT, Bank Local Business	C	211
SOCIAL STUDIES	Publishers	✓		✓				✓✓	✓✓	Printer/Publisher BBC Careers Scotland	P F	213
SOCIAL STUDIES	Sales Drive			✓				✓✓	✓	Business Advisor Charities Higher Education	P F C	215

Curricular Areas

TOPIC	Expressive Art	Health and Wellbeing	Language	Mathematics	RME	Science	Social Studies	Technologies	PARTNERS LINKS	AUDIENCE	Page No.
Enterprise through Craft	✓		✓				✓	✓✓	Local Business Suppliers Social Work Department	P B	219
Funding a Project	✓✓		✓	✓			✓✓	✓✓	Business Representative Local Entrepreneur Careers Scotland Bank Manager	P	221
Rapid Prototyping	✓			✓				✓✓	University Department University Liaison Officer	B P	223
Surfing the Waves			✓	✓			✓✓	✓✓	Local Businesses	P F	225
Marketing a Business	✓		✓					✓✓	Local Business FE	P	227

TECHNOLOGIES

Expressive Arts

- **Art & Design**

- **Music**

- **Drama**

Brief description
Organise an exhibition of work for an external audience.

"Enterprising" it!

1. **How we made learning *relevant* by putting into a *real context***
Exhibition was designed and layout organised by pupils.

Each pupil was allocated space in a "gallery" to fill with their completed works. Invitations which were designed by pupils, were extended to all staff, parents and families and to associated primary schools.

A catalogue was created using ideas from commercial galleries.

2. **How we encouraged pupils to take *responsibility***
The responsibility of pupils was to:
- finish and mount the work ready for the exhibition
- decide on a creative title for each work for inclusion in the catalogue
- organise the exhibition
- design invitations
- send out invitations
- host the event.

Curricular Areas

3. **How we involved partners in learning – building *relationships***
   External = Pupils made contact with the following:
   - All parents and members of the local community were invited to the opening of the exhibition
   - The local newspaper was informed of the event
   - Local gallery curators/Art Gallery professionals.

   Internal = other adults in school
   - All members of staff (teaching and non teaching) were invited to the opening.

4. **How we *reflected* on its success – assessment**
   The pupils exhibiting viewed the finished works in the gallery and, using set criteria, completed peer and self assessment.

   Teachers were given the opportunity to have one-to-one discussion with individuals suggesting ways to develop the performance further

   Pupils also evaluated their personal learning through the self evaluation process.

5. *Review* **– further ideas for development**
   - To run an exhibition and Sale of Work
   - To organise exhibitions for other year groups/primary schools
   - To provide a platform for local artists to exhibit and sell their work
   - To stage an exhibition at community venues
   - To consider links with other schools and with the local College of Further Education.

Brief description
Pupils had previously had the support of an Artist in Residence who worked in the school for one year. They wanted to celebrate the success of this initiative by putting on a Fashion Show.

"Enterprising" it!

---

1. **How we made learning *relevant* by putting into a *real context***
    - Pupils made jewellery as part of a topic in class
    - They organised a jewellery fashion show to exhibit their work
    - After discussion with the Headteacher it was decided to hold the event during the Induction Evening for parents of Primary 7 pupils
    - "Advanced Higher" pupils showcased their composition of music during the evening
    - Media Studies pupils honed their film making and technical skills.

---

2. **How we encouraged pupils to take *responsibility***
    Pupils decided how they would organise the following:
    - How to showcase their work
    - Programme for the evening
    - Models
    - Make-up
    - Poster production
    - Composing the music
    - Filming
    - Raffle
    - Hosting the event
    - Organising drinks and snacks.

Curricular Areas

---

3. **How we involved partners in learning – building *relationships***
   External = Business/Community/Parents & Families
   - Local artists presenting
   - Local Authority project which placed contemporary artists in residence at four schools. Specialisms included: silver, wood, textiles and ceramics
   - Parents/families: strengthening links, establishing new contact.

   Internal = Other adults in school
   - Art & Design Department
   - Music Department
   - Media Studies Department

4. **How we *reflected* on its success – assessment**
   - Feedback on the evening: verbal and written – from pupils and staff
   - Demand for more shows
   - Evaluation of the evening: handouts to parents, pupils and staff. Analysis for comments by pupils
   - Money raised for future projects in Art & Design Department
   - Assessment of personal learning.

5. ***Review* – further ideas for development**
   - To complete this project next year and expand upon it
   - Further collaboration expected between the Music and Art Departments.
   - Invite interest from other departments
   - Invite sponsorship from local businesses.

Curricular Areas

Sustainable design

Brief description
The pupils produced a design for a eco-friendly greenhouse for school/community use for a site on the school grounds. This is a Standard Grade design unit which involves building design.

"Enterprising" it!

---

1. **How we made learning *relevant* by putting into a *real context***
   Integral to this project is a real site and a real need. The "client" is the school and local community. The unit was made more enterprising by
   - Involvement of professionals: architect, planner, gardener
   - Investigation of other existing solutions
   - Meeting with representatives of potential community users
   - Using a problem-solving creative approach.

   Pupils, as part of their investigation, were required to identify and consult with potential project partners as well as with potential users of the facility.

   Visits were made to sites, including a geodesic dome and an earthship. Individuals researched building styles and technologies.

   The most successful design was taken forward and, led to a school/community project which set-up a market garden project.

---

2. **How we encouraged pupils to take *responsibility***
   Pupils were responsible for:
   - research into requirements
   - compiling and analysing information
   - preparing a design brief and presenting to an audience
   - contacting advisers, suppliers and customers.

---

3. **How we involved partners in learning – building *relationships***
   External = Business/Community/Parents & Families
   - Through contact with Royal Institute of Architects the services of two architects were solicited
   - A designer of buildings gave a presentation on sustainable building
   - Local Authority planning officers visited and spoke to pupils
   - School and community council representatives had a number of meetings with pupils.

   Internal = Other adults in school
   - Staff in other departments with an interest in using the greenhouse as a teaching facility were involved in meetings with pupils
   - The Departments of Biology, Technology and Physics, all who had an interest in the eco-technologies involved
   - Staff member offered clerk of works experience from previous career
   - The janitors also played key advisory roles.

4. **How we *reflected* on its success – assessment**
   Initial assessment was in presenting the work to SQA as part of coursework for Standard Grade Art & Design

   Pupils reflected on how their knowledge of subjects was in this real context.

5. ***Review* – further ideas for development**
   - This unit can easily be adapted to meet a range of needs on the building front
   - Schools can visibly show a commitment to ecological sustainability
   - Involve pupils in the design of projects such as bike sheds, shelters and gardens.

Brief description
Pupils worked with professional musicians to create and record their own piece of music. The CDs were sold to raise money for charity.

"Enterprising" it!

---

1. **How we made learning *relevant* by putting into a *real context***
   Pupils worked with professional musicians to create a piece of music based on stimulus materials.

   They had to consider their potential audience, their existing skills, the availability of instruments, and time constraints.

   Pupils learned about professional recording, about the equipment used, of the need to exclude external noise, and of having to re-record – just as in real life.

   They produced a professional CD for a real audience.

---

2. **How we encouraged pupils to take *responsibility***
   Pupils had responsibility for working with adults in the profession:
   - deciding on the type of music
   - choosing the instruments they would use
   - creating the length of the piece
   - choosing who would play which parts.

   Pupils took responsibility in the second part of the task by:
   - designing and producing the CD label
   - marketing of the product
   - selling CDs
   - monitoring finances.

Curricular Areas

3. **How we involved partners in learning – building *relationships***

External = Pupils made contact with the following:

- A co-ordinator and musicians from a local professional music company
- A recording engineer
- A local businessman, who gave advice on product design and hosted a visit and discussions with his company's graphic designers.

Internal = other adults in school

- The Music Department supported the first part of the project ie creating the piece
- The Business Education Department staff gave advice on costing, pricing and marketing
- The Art Department was involved in the design of the CD label
- Senior pupils and ICT staff supported the production of the CD labels and the copying of the CDs.

4. **How we *reflected* on its success – assessment**

Pupils assessed their learning of subject content in a real life situation and in how their knowledge was applied.

Pupils assessed their learning of business start up processes.

Pupils assessed their own learning on a personal level and what they had gained from the process.

5. ***Review* – further ideas for development**

- Working with other pupils on a specific theme eg Christmas songs.
- Linking with other year groups or schools in a bigger project.
- Using resource to raise awareness at Parents' Evenings, school shows, local and, national events.

Brief description
A singing and live band music production programme.

An extra-curricular activity designed to support, encourage and nurture musical talent.

Both programmes will lead to community performances in school, in other schools and in community venues.

"Enterprising" it!

1. **How we made learning *relevant* by putting into a *real context***

   We invited a group of well-known local singers to perform to the whole school and ran a series of workshops on singing coaching and presenting performances on stage.

   In addition, the school employed the services of a Community Music Therapist to work with a group of 20 young people, one day per week after school.

   This culminated in a real event which was a musical evening production run and organised by the pupils.

2. **How we encouraged pupils to take *responsibility***

   The young participants took responsibility for :
   - choosing their own backing tracks on instrumental pieces
   - supporting and encouraging one another
   - selecting opportunities for performance learning
   - designing advertising materials
   - planning the event
   - identifying and inviting an audience
   - helping set up electronic equipment
   - organising refreshments
   - ensuring the evening was successful.

Curricular Areas

3. **How we involved partners in learning – building *relationships***
    External = Business / Community / Parents & Families
    - Local musical professionals
    - Community Music Therapist
    - To seek external funding, we formed partnerships with Social Work, Police, voluntary agencies, and the private sector
    - At our first concert invitations were extended to parents and families of the young people, along with our partner organisations.

    Internal = Other adults in school
    - We were supported by the Senior Management Team, who visited the performing workshops.

4. **How we *reflected* on its success – assessment**
    - By quantifying the number of young people continually attending the workshops and extra-curricular activities – 95%
    - By quantifying the number of tickets sold or given away for performance, 60/150, 1st month
    - Through conversations with pupils and parents.
    - By tracking the number of invitations to perform three concerts now booked within the community over the coming months.
    - Pupils assessed their learning of subject content and application to real life situation: discussion and evaluation activities
    - Pupils assessed their personal learning – self-awareness, teamwork, creativity, achievement, success and confidence
    - Pupils evaluated their part in the business process.

5. ***Review* – further ideas for development**
    - To provide recording studio opportunities
    - To develop a pathway to future learning opportunities
    - To introduce young people to professional musicians with a view to performance opportunities
    - To increase media coverage.

© Enterprising Careers, University of Strathclyde, 2007.

Brief description

Pupils organised and took part in a live music performance/workshop in the school's Music Department. The purpose was to give pupils opportunities in the music sector and to allow them to experience what it is like to be a professional musician.

"Enterprising" it!

1. **How we made learning *relevant* by putting into a *real context***

   The audience was our string pupils, piano pupils, string pupils from our associated primaries, Standard Grade pupils, Higher & Advanced Higher pupils and pupils from our wind band.

   Pupils were able to hear a live performance and take part in workshop.

   Pupils prepared questions and found out more about the life of a musician – career possibilities and pathways were discussed.

2. **How we encouraged pupils to take *responsibility***

   Pupils took responsibility for:
   - marketing the event
   - planning the event
   - organising arrangements for the day
   - inviting associated primary schools
   - taking part in the discussions
   - follow-up activities eg. thank you letters.

   Pupils co-operated with each other and with members of staff to ensure the smooth running of the event.

Curricular Areas

3. **How we involved partners in learning – building *relationships***
   External = Business/Community/Parents & Families
   - A well-known local quartet were assisted by the Chamber Music Society and Enterprise Music Scotland
   - Within the community we involved our associated primaries and invited the primary pupils to come into their secondary school and work with our pupils
   - Parents were invited to attend and participate.

   Internal = Other adults in school
   - We brought the instrumental service into the classroom via our string teacher and all music staff were present at performance.
   - Adults came from primary schools with primary pupils.

4. **How we *reflected* on its success – assessment**

   - Staff assessed pupils' learning of subject – positive response
   - Pupils wrote a report on the impact of the venture
   - The learning experience was evaluated for Enterprise Music Scotland
   - Pupils assessed their own learning on a personal level – career opportunities, self awareness, co-operation and creativity.

5. ***Review* – further ideas for development**
   - We hope to provide similar activities for other disciplines in the schools.
   - We have organised a similar event for "brass" and "woodwind" sections.
   - We will work in partnership with another local secondary school. Pupils are already planning next steps.

Brief description
Putting techniques into practice by directing a drama production.

"Enterprising" it!

1. **How we made learning *relevant* by putting into a *real context***
   Our target for this unit was to investigate the fun of Melodrama Theatre. We wanted to learn the techniques, and put them into practice. By experimenting with these techniques the pupils had a deeper understanding of the era. It was made 'real' because they put on performances for other classes.

2. **How we encouraged pupils to take *responsibility***
   The class selected groups and a Director was selected from within each group. Each group had an individual responsibility for its own productions.

   They had to "block" their actors, take their group through a melodrama script and take responsibility for the organisation of the entire performance.

   The actors took responsibility for their active role by learning their scripts and taking direction, as in real life.

Curricular Areas

3. How we involved partners in learning – building *relationships*

External = Business/Community/Parents & Families

- We staged a performance for parents and families in order to highlight the work of the department and to promote the talents of the young people
- Local theatre company.

Internal = Other adults in school

- We invited other classes and teachers to be the audience for performances.

4. How we *reflected* on its success – assessment

After each period each person would evaluate his/her own role/performance and that of the others. After each performance the other groups would become "theatre critics", evaluating both strengths and weaknesses.

The class also did a written evaluation on the way in which they used effective melodrama techniques.

5. *Review* – further ideas for development

- Bigger final performances
- A trip to see a professional performance of this type of theatre
- Widening the audience: to the local wider community
- Develop marketing techniques to reach potential audiences outwith the school community
- Seek sponsorship from within local business community.

Health & Wellbeing

- **Physical Education**
- **Home Economics**
- **Personal & Social Development**

Brief description
Encouraging physical activity and promoting health through Music, ICT and group work.

This programme was developed by a Music Therapy Support Team as a way of resolving non-participation issues.

"Enterprising" it!

1. **How we made learning *relevant* by putting into a *real context***
   The participants were introduced to each other during a "music therapy session". Group discussions took place during a series of workshops where it was established what a particular group of girls were finding difficult about PE.

   Ideas were generated by the group to ascertain what direction they would take. Issues surrounding participation in PE were discussed

   The girls took ownership and responsibility for developing a new approach to Health and Fitness, and affecting a change in their attitude to physical activity.

   A programme was put in place after liaison with the PE Department and Music Therapy Support Team.

2. **How we encouraged pupils to take *responsibility***
   The young participants took responsibility by:
   - supporting each other's development
   - finding opportunities to develop a healthier lifestyle
   - organising out of school trips to fitness centres
   - researching the benefits of exercise and healthy living using ICT
   - designing questionnaires for PE teachers, female workers at leisure centres and 5th year PE pupils asking why they choose healthy lifestyle/careers.

Curricular Areas

3. **How we involved partners in learning – building *relationships***
   External = Business / Community / Parents & Families
   - Community health workers
   - Drug/alcohol educators
   - Other professionals who facilitated discussions on the topics and issues previously agreed by the group
   - Visit to the local Leisure Centre.

   Internal = Other adults in school
   - Liaison and ongoing communication between PE Department and Music Therapy Support Team
   - Female health professional for women's health discussions.

4. **How we *reflected* on its success – assessment**
   - 100% attendance every week
   - Girls demonstrated real motivation during the sessions
   - In conversation with the girls, they expressed an interest in doing more work on chosen areas - subject content was effectively addressed
   - Girls assessed their personal learning – confidence, self awareness, working together, achieving, communication.

5. ***Review* – further ideas for development**
   - Possible development of women's health programme for 13 – 15 year olds
   - Look at the reasons for non-participation with the PE department and possible solutions to encourage full participation
   - Pupils organise and run a health awareness event – involving local sportsmen and women to promote and raise the profile of the importance of health & fitness.

Brief description

Group Dance –choreographed by pupils and presented to each other before recording the dance on video which was viewed by other pupils and by parents to demonstrate work being carried out in the department and to use to develop new projects.

"Enterprising" it!

1. **How we made learning *relevant* by putting into a *real context***
    We used expertise gained in class to present to an audience of peers, parents and other students, primary classes and parents. We demonstrated skills development as a display of work whilst giving purpose to learning and using the opportunity for the class to achieve success and confidence. In this way they showed how they engaged with learning.

    Each 'group' within the class created a piece of work and gave 'mini' performances.

    The focus of this approach was a presentation of dance skills.

    All groups in the whole dance show worked as a team to ensure the smooth running of the performance.

2. **How we encouraged pupils to take *responsibility***
    Pupils took responsibility for:
    *   working with a partner to decide on and create a routine to be incorporated into the main dance.
    *   co-ordinating with their sub-group
    *   organising all aspects of this show
    *   managing the music as they worked
    *   organising props
    *   filming the final performance
    *   editing the video for use

3. **How we involved partners in learning – building *relationships***
   Extent = Business/Community/Parents & Families
   - Professional dance group – to demonstrate a performance
   - Local dance school to discuss techniques, choreography, and filming
   - Video producer to advise on aspects of production
   - Parents to view video at Parents' Evenings.

   Internal = Other adults in school –
   - Music Department
   - Media staff
   - Drama teacher
   - Technician.

---

4. **How we *reflected* on its success – assessment**
   We discussed how we had benefited from this experience.
   Pupils learned techniques in dance and applied their knowledge in a real situation.

   Pupils also developed skills in:
   - Organisation
   - Communication
   - Presentation
   - Confidence building
   - Problem solving
   - Working with others.

---

5. ***Review* – further ideas for development**
   - A similar dance project next session to be shown to visiting Primary 7 pupils as an example of pupil work in S1
   - Present their work at future Parents' Evenings
   - Part of a school show/display of work
   - Plan, organise and run a school/community dance show.

Brief description

Pupils planned, organized and prepared a meal for parents and carers, teachers and friends, replicating how a restaurant works.

"Enterprising" it!

1. **How we made learning *relevant* by putting into a *real context***
    Audience: Headteacher, Depute Head Teachers, Teachers, Parents and Carers, Friends

    Action: After a 10 week period of in-house training at a local hotel, pupils planned, organised and prepared dinner for 25 people. The pupils were guided by the hotel chef through the various stages of investigating, planning, making and evaluating.

    Relevance: Experience of working in a real life situation and working environment. Gaining insight into how the hospitality industry works in relation to school learning.

    REHIS (Royal Environmental Health Institute of Scotland) Certificate.

2. **How we encouraged pupils to take *responsibility***
    Pupils were encouraged to take responsibility for their own personal hygiene and safety.

    Pupils generated ideas. They prepared, planned and organised the meal.

    Pupils took ownership: They had to design and make invitations for the event and ensure that they were sent out, received and had been replied to.

    Pupil co-operation: Pupils organised tasks and decided who would make which courses on the day. Depending on the task pupils worked independently or in a group.

Curricular Areas

3.   **How we involved partners in learning – building *relationships***

External - = Business / Community / Parents & Families

- Springboard – Pupils involved in Visit Scotland Discovery Trail – tour of restaurants, hotels in the vicinity of George Square and surrounding area
- Business - Pupils made contact with various members of hotel staff. Pupils given tour of hotel and met with housekeeping staff, bar/restaurant staff, porters, kitchen staff and reception staff
- Pupils invited teachers, friends and parents to dinner at hotel
- Local press were involved in taking photographs and in highlighting the event within the local community
- Video taken of whole day event by School Technician

Internal = other adults in school

- Teachers, parents and friends involved. Links were made with the P.E., H.E. and Modern Languages Departments. This project included these departments as it was part of the course. Modern Language input to broaden the pupils knowledge of culinary terminology, phrases and sayings that would help in understanding of working in the hospitality industry.

4.   **How we *reflected* on its success – assessment**

- We looked at what we had learned and achieved from this project and believe that it had been a worthwhile, valuable, experience for the pupils.

The pupils used many skills in this experience such as:

- Working on their own. Relating what they enjoyed/didn't enjoy about the course
- Working with others. Pupils discussed problems/experience gained, positive aspects of hospitality industry
- Working as a whole team.
- Being able to plan, prepare, organise and put the skills learned into practice in a real context.

5.   *Review* **– further ideas for development**

- Link up with hotel or hotel/cookery school abroad to broaden horizons
- Increase time spent at hotel each week (if possible)
- Depending on what country we visited, do cross curricular work with Modern Languages Department to strengthen that particular language
- Link with Business Education to look at business skills required – finances (profit, costing, supplies, etc), marketing, and customer care

Design and make activity

Brief description
Pupils were given a design brief. Based on their knowledge and skills gained in subject area they had to design and make a lunch dish suitable for selling in the school dining room.

Their final product was analysed and judged by a panel of experts against set criteria.

"Enterprising" it!

1. **How we made learning *relevant* by putting into a *real context***
There has been a great deal of attention in the media recently on the poor diet of many children. Concern has been expressed about quality and nutritional value of foods provided in school dining halls.

   The challenge was to put their learning into a real life context by designing a suitable dish to be included in the school lunch menu. Criteria set by the experts included nutritional value, cost, production methods, storage and mass appeal. They had to work within a limited budget and comply with a healthy eating policy.

   Pupils carried out research into what foods pupils eat. By using their research findings they were then in a position to design and make a dish. This was produced, sampled and evaluated against the above criteria. Their audience were the experts as well as the rest of the school as the winning dish was prepared in the school canteen and served during lunch.

2. **How we encouraged pupils to take *responsibility***
Pupils decided on procedure and assumed roles within groups.
Pupils met with the school cook and viewed the canteen facilities.
Pupils carried out two investigations, gathering and analysing information:
from pupils/staff/ food preparation and staff advisors.

   Pupils planned, analysed, designed, and made a lunch dish. Trials were organised and they reflected on what had been produced. Pupils then evaluated their work. They presented to the experts who judged the winner.

Curricular Areas

3. **How we involved partners in learning – building *relationships***

   External = Business/Community/Parents & Families

   Information was sourced from a variety of experts:

   - Food production manager
   - Food sales manager
   - Nutritionist
   - Chef
   - Local Authority Schools Meals Provision Advisor.

   Internal = Other adults in school

   - Meetings with Catering Officer.
   - Questionnaires completed by members of staff/parents/pupils
   - Members of staff and S4 pupils on judging panel.

4. **How we *reflected* on its success – assessment**

   They demonstrated that the learning was more effective than theoretical learning. Pupils produced some amazing research findings which enabled them to design a healthy lunch.

   Students were asked to prepare a short report reviewing their task – stating how challenges were met and reflecting upon the success of their product.

   They also assessed their personal learning such as ability to work with others, self-awareness, effective communication skills, creativity, synthesising information.

5. ***Review* – further ideas for development**

   - Packed lunch options for primary pupils
   - Similar process to develop products for sale in local businesses
   - Visit from local chef to outline the process used in a restaurant to design and make new additions to a menu
   - This unit will be extended to incorporate a visit to a local hotel kitchen to experience the workings of a 'real' kitchen.

Product Development

Brief description
Pupils were challenged to develop an innovative product to enhance their business partners' product range.
A competition judged by a team of experts.

"Enterprising" it!

1. **How we made learning *relevant* by putting into a *real context***

   All S2 pupils teamed up with a real business partner who provided products for Marks and Spencer. Workshops featured job remits, product development and marketing.

   The winning teams took part in a local competition.

   The audience was the business partner who may further develop the idea for their customers.

   Aims: – to establish direct links between the skills learned in Home Economics and those required by food manufacturers.
   Relevance: - Experiencing the commercial side of Food Product Development.

2. **How we encouraged pupils to take *responsibility***

   Pupils were set the task and divided themselves into teams. Ideas from pupils were collated.

   They took responsibility for analysing the brief, carrying out the research over several weeks in school and at home, writing a specification and developing a solution. They created and named their dish, planned their time, cooked and served the dish to maximise appeal.

   All dishes were made and tested and ingredients amended if necessary.
   Teachers and other pupils gave constructive feedback.

   Pupils designed an eye-catching label for their product. This included researching the nutritional values for their dish using ICT to ensure a professional looking product.

---

3. **How we involved partners in learning – building *relationships***
External = Pupils made contact with the following:

- Parents - for advice/research
- Business Partner – provided support financially and judged the final in school
- Supermarket staff during research phase
- Local media invited along with a councillor to attend the final and take photographs
- External competition for winning teams.

Internal = other adults in school.

- Computing Department – production of the food labels
- Art & Design - food labels/judges for each practical class final
- Headteacher/Depute Head – judged on final day
- School Board/Parents/Staff – all informed through the school newsletter.

4. **How we *reflected* on its success – assessment**
Pupils reflected on success overall – by assessing individuals' skills. Relevance of school work to employment opportunities.

Coverage in local newspapers, school newsletter and awareness-raising around the school.

Impact on learning - more depth, motivation, co-operation and better understanding of the relevance of the subject to the world of business.

Food Product Development Unit –this competition has had an enormous impact on our pupils by motivating them and so increasing numbers in S3.

5. ***Review* – further ideas for development**
- Development of relationship with business partner
- Visits from school staff and pupils to business premises
- Liaising with pupils in 'Hospitality' class and business partner.

Brief description
The emphasis in this project is on teaching practical skills for use in industry and in preparation for employment.

"Enterprising" it!

1. **How we made learning *relevant* by putting into a *real context***
   S2 pupils were put in a situation resembling a real restaurant:
   - Each event was a practical lesson around preparing food for the public. This included skills of food preparation techniques, cooking skills, and involved an understanding of health and safety rules and food hygiene
   - Linked to the Hospitality Industry
   - Equipment and resources were used which would not normally be used in an Home Economics Department ie. specialist catering equipment
   - Pupils were given chefs' whites and hats to replicate a realistic hospitality setting.

2. **How we encouraged pupils to take *responsibility***
   - Pupils took responsibility for their own attendance at the eight week programme as an extra curricular activity
   - Pupils were encouraged at all stages to co-operate and work with others
   - Pupils were given responsibility for use of equipment and hygiene rules
   - Pupils had responsibility for producing a dish from a recipe.

Curricular Areas

3. **How we involved partners in learning – building *relationships***

External - = Business / Community / Parents & Families

- A chef from the local college was an invited guest. All resources were provided by college. Link was made with FE and therefore possible future training on leaving school. Awards made to students on completion
- The Careers Advisors discussed career opportunities with the group
- Parents were invited along to final session to share in learning.

Internal = Other adults in school

- Other staff were invited to watch the demonstrations.

---

4. **How we *reflected* on its success – assessment**

- Pupils were involved in changing recipes for the next group ie. this recipe could be made better by . . .
- Pupils were also asked to generate ideas for future subjects
- Pupils considered what they had gained from the experience – learning of topic content, skills development, industry experience
- Pupils evaluated their personal skills development – self awareness, working with others, creativity, flexibility, achievement.

---

5. ***Review* – further ideas for development**

- This will run again from next week
- We have decided to open this up to S2, S3 and S4 pupils to allow pupils to mix with other year groups as well as having a built in peer support group
- The theme will be Healthy Eating as this will tie in the work being taught within the department.

Brief description
Pupils prepared a presentation to P7 providing guidance on safe routes to High School.

"Enterprising" it!

1. **How we made learning *relevant* by putting into a *real context***
   - This is a real situation as P7 pupils must be provided with this very important information before beginning the new session at High School
   - S1 pupils have personal experience of this and can research the topic further to provide depth of information
   - 12 Tutor Groups (20 pupils in each) competed for a prize under the umbrella of citizenship
   - Each group had to make a presentation to a panel of judges
   - This information was then presented by selected groups to P7 pupils at Induction Event.

2. **How we encouraged pupils to take *responsibility***
   - Pupils selected their groups and their roles within those groups
   - Pupils researched the topic by gathering and analysing information through market research/internet/ discussions
   - Pupils decided on the method and content of their presentation
   - Pupils organised themselves by delegating tasks and timescales
   - Core materials and instructions were provided; additional props were left for pupils to arrange
   - Pupils planned, produced and prepared their presentations.

Curricular Areas

3. **How we involved partners in learning – building *relationships***
External = Business / Community / Parents & Families
- Health Promoting Schools
- Transport Department
- Road Safety Unit
- Community Police
- Community Council
- Primary School
- Local Media

Internal = Other adults in school
- Twelve S1 Tutors, Principal Teacher of Pupil Support/ PSD, Head of Year, Sports Co-ordinator, Depute Headteacher, Janitor, Crossing Assistants, Classroom Assistants.

4. **How we *reflected* on its success – assessment**
- Final presentations to panel of judges. Criteria set – content, relevance, style, recognition of dangers and benefits
- Winning presentation was used for P7 pupils. Winning group chose to go on a trip to a Safari Park
- Teachers assessed impact of learning using this approach (ownership of project) over traditional approach (provision of information)
- Pupils assessed their own learning on a personal level – i.e. more confidence, improved interpersonal skills, improved communication skills more responsible attitudes, effective citizens.

5. ***Review* – further ideas for development**
- Annual event planned as part of the transition process
- All primary schools in cluster to be involved next year
- Production of a website to enable all associated primaries to be involved in the process
- Production of a newsletter or leaflet.

Brief description
Pupils took part in an environmental project to improve various aspects of the school.

"Enterprising" it!

1. **How we made learning *relevant* by putting into a *real context***
   The aim of this exercise was to give pupils ownership of their school and its environment and to encourage them to develop ideas for improving the school. These ideas were submitted for implementation to the Senior Management Team.

   Audience
   - Peers, Pupil Council, Visitors, Headteacher and other pupils

   Action
   - Information gathering about the school environment – photographs, questionnaires and interviews
   - Looking at ideas for improvement and choosing best options
   - Planning the changes.
   - Presentations to peers.

   Relevance
   - Appreciation of the school and the environment
   - Understanding that pupils themselves can affect a change
   - Realisation of the "responsible citizenship" role each plays within the school community.

2. **How we encouraged pupils to take *responsibility***
   Pupils worked in groups to:
   - list all the positive aspects of the school environment
   - identify areas for improvement
   - identify one area where they felt they could make a difference
   - identify an area for improvement and undertook to write letters, interview relevant people, compile questionnaires and collate information.

   Pupils assumed roles in order to take ideas forward and improve the school environment.

Curricular Areas

3. How we involved partners in learning – building *relationships*

External = Business / Community / Parents & Families

- Pupils wrote letters to the local council to ask for help with recycling waste
- They wrote to the local authority Catering Manager to elicit his views on "Healthy Eating" and" Hungry for Success" strategies
- Contacted Land Services at local council.

Internal = Other adults in school

Letters were written to:

- The Headteacher
- The Kitchen Supervisor
- The Pupil Council.

The following were interviewed:

- The Headteacher
- The Kitchen Supervisor.

4. How we *reflected* on its success – assessment

- Pupils presented their findings using PowerPoint presentation and poster display
- Groups were assessed and a discussion took place on how well they thought they had worked as a group/as individuals
- Pupils completed an evaluation sheet (individually) on how they felt they had worked in the group and what skills and qualities they had brought to the project
- Pupils assessed their personal learning – achievement, participation, etc.

5. *Review* – further ideas for development

- Some excellent ideas came out of this initiative and they have all been submitted to the Pupil Council for discussion and possible future implementation
- It is hoped that some of the presentations could be used in Year Group Assembly
- Submit ideas to local Community Council meetings
- Give a presentation at the next local 'Youth Forum'.

Curricular Areas

Languages

- **English**

- **Gaelic**

- **Modern Languages**

Brief description
The project was aimed at improving pupils writing. The pupils' writing skills improved a great deal, largely as a result of increased motivation and a realistic context for the project.
Pupils filmed a re-enactment of a chosen text.

"Enterprising" it!

1. **How we made learning *relevant* by putting into a *real context***
   Flour Babies Project – an enterprising unit for the novel *"Flour Babies"* by author Anne Fine.

   The book is about an 'unsettled' class which is required to participate in a science experiment where they must each care for a 'flour baby'. In order to gain a better understanding of how this novel was written pupils re-enacted the book and wrote their own accounts. They completed a report (functional), drama script (creative) diary (personal).

   The pupils were filmed throughout the project and a "movie" was the result, which was viewed at a national film theatre.

2. **How we encouraged pupils to take *responsibility***
   Pupils had to work together as a team to provide the 'baby' with appropriate care. The group with the highest points tally (based on a pre-selected set of criteria) was the eventual winner.

   The fact that pupils shared a baby in a team encouraged them to take responsibility – their actions affected not only themselves but their team members.

   They also had responsibility for writing a personalised account of their experience. Each pupil was required to keep a 'baby diary' which they shared with their group. Each pupil wrote a final report on the project (functional writing).

Curricular Areas

3. How we involved partners in learning – building *relationships*

External = Business/Community/Parents & Families

- Parents/Business reps/local authority employees were invited to a screening of our movie – *Flour Babies:* The Movie – at the Glasgow Film Theatre
- Director of Film Theatre – advice – guidance.

Internal = Other adults in school

- Classroom/SEN assistants worked with *all* pupils to participate in all aspects of the project, from report writing to filming.

---

4. How we *reflected* on its success – assessment

Each group wrote an evaluation of the various aspects of the project – responses were filed and included on final cut of 'movie'.

Pupils assessed their personal learning – self-awareness, working with others, and problem solving.

---

5. *Review* – further ideas for development

- This year, the teacher took responsibility for editing the movie. It would now be appropriate for this to be a process undertaken by members of the class who have been involved in the initial filming of the footage.
- Use this process with other novels, topics to enhance learning.
- Involvement of other departments.

Curricular Areas

Brief description

Groups to prepare and make speeches on local community issues to a panel of Business/ Community representatives who judged the competition.

Presentations were used by local media and for use in local community.

"Enterprising" it!

---

1. **How we made learning *relevant* by putting into a *real context***
    Pupils were challenged with writing an article on a subject of their choice about their local community and then preparing information and presenting the information to a panel of judges from a local community committee.

    They were assessed on content, clarity, humour and presentation.

    The presentations were displayed in the local community and used in the local and school newsletters to outline issues relevant to all and to give a young person's perception of the issue.

---

2. **How we encouraged pupils to take *responsibility***
    Initially pupils generated ideas on topics and wrote an article about an issue of interest to them.

    Then pupils worked in groups and took responsibility for:
    *   discussing the value of each and deciding upon their group theme
    *   researching information around the topic
    *   compiling information
    *   preparing information for presentation
    *   participating in the presentation.

---

3. How we involved partners in learning – building *relationships*

External = Business/Community/Parents & Families

- Local business/ community groups who provided advice and guidance and agreed to participate as judges
- Local media involved in recording and including presentations.

Internal = Other adults in school

- All members of staff received invitations to the presentation event
- Other class members/year members attended the presentation event.

---

4. How we *reflected* on its success – assessment

The class felt that they had learned a lot eg. more understanding of issues in the community; more understanding of values and community perceptions.

They gained knowledge, understanding, confidence and enjoyment from the activity.

This learning was assessed and recorded – both on personal learning gains and working with others.

---

5. *Review* – further ideas for development

- Visit the Scottish Parliament or Local Sheriff Court to witness 'debate'
- Perhaps all focus on similar issue but have different points of view
- Visit a committee meeting and see how a real one worked.

© Enterprising Careers, University of Strathclyde, 2007.

Brief description

To encourage creative and original thinking, through the task of designing a Children's Storybook.

"Enterprising" it!

1. **How we made learning *relevant* by putting into a *real context***
   Pupils were challenged with
   - writing
   - illustrating
   - producing a storybook for primary age children.

   The groups were judged upon:
   - Original story
   - Illustrations
   - Creativity
   - Product design
   - Co-operative working.

   The final products would be assessed and the best would be displayed in the local bookshop.

2. **How we encouraged pupils to take *responsibility***
   Pupils worked in groups and took responsibility for:

   - generating ideas for theme
   - researching information around the topic
   - working co-operatively to produce the book
   - compiling information – through use of ICT
   - managing their time for the task
   - writing the story – careful use of language for specific age group
   - illustrating effectively and appropriately
   - preparing the cover for the book
   - outline a marketing plan for sale and use of book.

Curricular Areas

3. **How we involved partners in learning – building *relationships***

   External = Business/Community/Parents & Families
   - Local book shop who displayed their work
   - Primary teachers/parents who provided advice and guidance and agreed to participate as judges
   - Local business who gave a talk on authors, books, appeal, selling, target market, etc
   - Graphic designer who gave advice on book design / illustrations
   - Primary pupils/families who 'tested' the products.

   Internal = Other adults in school
   - Each group had a senior pupil as a facilitator to assist them with their task
   - Art, ICT Departments.

4. **How we *reflected* on its success – assessment**

   Skills developed in book production, sense of purpose for writing, confidence and enjoyment from the activity.

   The pupils assessed their own learning – what they had gained from the experience.

   Feedback from primary schools and from families on their products.

5. ***Review* – further ideas for development**
   - Need to allocate more time to event
   - Focus on another age group / topic

Brief description

Students chose a topic relevant to the course work and made a 5 minute presentation to an audience in a language other than English.

"Enterprising" it!

1. **How we made learning *relevant* by putting into a *real context***
    The audience was the class.

    Students researched their own topic and presented their findings in the foreign language.

    The students shared their knowledge via their presentation (using PowerPoint) and leaflets.

    All students produced a PowerPoint presentation which included pictures, tables and diagrams as aids to their speaking.

2. **How we encouraged pupils to take *responsibility***
    As a class we initially discussed different topic options. Students, in groups, were encouraged to come up with their own ideas and decide how to do the research, assuming roles and responsibilities to achieve the task.

    Students were also encouraged to support each other and share resources.

Curricular Areas

3. How we involved partners in learning – building *relationships*

External = Business / Community / Parents & Families

- Students were encouraged to create questionnaires to gather information/opinions relevant to their topic and these were given to appropriate groups ie. other students, teachers, parents, community or companies
- When questionnaires were used they were frequently sent by email to the relevant people.

Internal = Other adults in school

- All adults in school were invited to lunchtime information sessions to raise the profile of the work within the school.

4. How we *reflected* on its success – assessment

Did the presentation satisfy the criteria to pass Scottish Qualifications Authority (SQA) assessment (NAB)?

Following the presentation, students had to take part in a 6 minute question and answer session where half the time was taken up by Personal Study (presentation). It gave the teacher the opportunity to assess the students' opinions on their study, the difficulties they had encountered and on their achievement.

Assessment focused on independent learning strategies not only consolidation of knowledge/understanding of topic but also on their transferable skills such as communication, working with others, creativity, confidence and achievement.

5. *Review* – further ideas for development

- Linking up with their peer groups in other schools working on projects together sharing information using ICT skills
- Involve native speakers to listen to and comment on individual presentations prior to formal assessment
- Appeal via newsletter and local press for volunteers within the community to help with the above. Raise profile of the Department at Parents' Evenings. Seek help from native speakers amongst parent groups.

Curricular Areas

Translating for local businesses

Brief description
Working with local cafes, pupils translated their menus into another language, to meet the emerging needs of the local tourist industry.

"Enterprising" it!

1. **How we made learning *relevant* by putting into a *real context***
   The pupils held meetings with local businesses to ascertain the project potential and gauge business interest and demand.

   The pupils applied their skills and knowledge of the subject to a real-life business situation, developing and delivering a professional product for use in the local community.

   Audience – business partners.

2. **How we encouraged pupils to take *responsibility***
   The project was organised and managed by the pupils.

   The challenges/responsibilities:
   - to create a professional product
   - to apply subject knowledge in a real situation and with a real audience
   - to gain understanding of how business works
   - to manage their time
   - co-operate as teams and with external partners
   - meet business expectations and deadlines
   - share responsibilities.

3. **How we involved partners in learning – building *relationships***
   External = Pupils made contact with the following:
   - Owners of each business.

   Internal = other adults in school
   - Foreign language assistants to ensure complete accuracy in the finished product
   - The Depute Rector
   - The Enterprise in Education (EiE) co-ordinator
   - Language teachers.

4. **How we *reflected* on its success – assessment**
   Pupils
   - Understanding of application of subject knowledge to business
   - Increase in personal skills = confidence, self-awareness, communication.

   Teachers
   - Impact on learning.

   Business
   - Impact on business
   - Potential for future school – business partnership working.

5. ***Review* – further ideas for development**
   - Display of knowledge to highlight work done
   - Presentations to Year Group Assemblies
   - Tourism in the locality – presenter from Tourist Board
   - Careers in the Tourist Industry
   - Liaison with Careers Adviser.

Curricular Areas

Exciting Cities!

Brief description
Developing language skills through research. Presenting information for tourists going to another country (and doing so in language of subject area).

"Enterprising" it!

1. **How we made learning *relevant* by putting into a *real context***
   Audience: Using the appropriate tourist board website and various associated links, an Internet challenge was set where pupils had to find information on visitor attractions, sites/monuments timetables and opening times of various exhibitions.

   Presentations were given to the rest of class and teacher on "Tourist advice for visitors".

---

2. **How we encouraged pupils to take *responsibility***
   There was whole class discussion to initially decide on information required. why it should be included and how to find it eg. how to use a search engine in order to find relevant sites of information.

   Pupils took ownership of the task by working in groups discussing places they would like to visit. They assumed roles and responsibilities for the tasks.

   They collated, analysed and chose relevant information and prepared a suitable presentation.

Curricular Areas

3. **How we involved partners in learning – building *relationships***

   External = Business/Community/Parents & Families

   - A parent who worked in the travel industry was invited to speak to the class about careers in this arena
   - Travel agent advised on the type of information tourists look for and how to present it effectively.

   Internal = Other adults in school – ICT department.

---

4. **How we *reflected* on its success – assessment**

   Reflection: Pupils discussed their problem-solving skills and found the task challenging and interesting. They also discussed how these skills would be transferable in order to organise trips/holidays to other destinations.

   Assessment: They assessed their success by researching and identifying points of interest with the help of a questionnaire regarding actual facts to be obtained, such as; - 1. The cost of the underground between stations. - 2. The height of a famous building – 3. Which museum houses which famous painting – 4. The price of entry to an exhibition.

   New vocabulary was consolidated and tested in the form of a class test.

   Pupils worked in pairs and discussed their transferable skills with a view to using them. They reflected on specific attributes such as leadership, listener, facilitator, motivator and co-ordinator.

---

5. ***Review* – further ideas for development**

   - Brochures with information on famous places to visit in a city
   - Information on travelling around and costs with a vocabulary section containing helpful phrases and cultural information
   - A challenge to be organised between twin school and our school where each has to find out information about each other's area
   - Wall display of knowledge; presentations by pupils at future school assemblies
   - Presence at local "education fair", where best practice is highlighted.
   - Trip to chosen city.

Brief description

We staged a Fashion Show in order to make the topic more 'enterprising', and in so doing, made the teaching of adjectives more enjoyable. This was integral to the course work – unit taught throughout.

"Enterprising" it!

1. **How we made learning *relevant* by putting into a *real context***

   Firstly, we made presentations to other groups in class in poster format, sharing our knowledge of French designers, the history of fashion, fashion houses and labels. We investigated the world of fashion through the media and the internet. Thereafter, we displayed our findings in classroom and corridors. Others became interested in what we were doing.

   As our confidence grew, we were keen to tell others about what we had learned. We made presentations to other classes in our year group, using posters and interactive white boards.

   We decided to create and describe our own outfits using our knowledge of French adjectives to describe what each group had designed. We expanded our knowledge of vocabulary for the topic.

   We then staged a Fashion Show, reaching a wider audience by speaking at year group assemblies. We planned, organised and marketed the event as a way of reaching parents and the business community. We set up a committee and involved other departments.

2. **How we encouraged pupils to take *responsibility***

   Setting the scene: a series of class subjects combined learning with the proposed project.

   We generated ideas to take the activity forward, deciding on the format, audience and roles and remits. Pupils became writers, artists, marketing executives, models, and film-makers and took ownership by designing outfits, and the programme.

   Pupils co-operated with each other by combining resources, carrying out tasks, assuming roles independently and in groups.

Curricular Areas

3. How we involved partners in learning – building *relationships*
External = Business / Community / Parents & Families
We invited local business people, such as a clothes manufacturer, designer and retailer to school to talk to pupils. Parents working in related industries were also included. We attracted sponsors from business and decided where the profits were to go. The local press was contacted and helped us greatly in our advertising strategy.

Internal = Other adults in school
We invited other departments to join our committee - Art, ICT, HE, Music and History. Links were made with PSD/ Guidance teachers, and the school Careers Adviser There were regular meetings with a member of the Senior Management Team to give updates on the focus and progress of the Fashion Show. We had slots at assemblies which were invaluable for marketing. The school newsletter featured information on our project and what we were learning, as did the school Intranet.

4. How we *reflected* on its success – assessment
We reflected on what had been learned. Consolidation of the topic was done in mini-tests and in end of unit assessment: vocabulary, adjectives (order – agreement, etc)

Evidence of development of enterprising skills was collected which were used in personal learning plans.
Self-assessment focused on the following statements:
I have made a decision: On my own
                    with another pupil
                    with a group of pupils
                    with the class
                    other people said I did it well

Working in a group: Find 4 words to describe your behaviour in most groups
                          Write about the kind of role you usually play
                          What do you do if there is a problem?
                          How would you improve the way you work in a group?

Personal qualities: I communicate easily
                          I am adaptable
                          I am a capable leader

See '*Up for Enterprise*' pack for further details.

5. *Review* – further ideas for development
- Video conferencing with school in France
- Debate on school uniform versus fashion wear
- Cross curricular annual event to incorporate French food and culture.

© Enterprising Careers, University of Strathclyde, 2007.

Making a DVD

Brief description
Production of a short DVD news programme encompassing all year groups. This was sold to schools and to the community to assist people in learning about language and culture and enabling them to feel more confident when visiting the country and its people.

"Enterprising" it!

1. **How we made learning *relevant* by putting into a *real context***
   We made a modern language news programme in DVD format which featured newscasters and a continuity announcer.

   We sold the completed DVDs as part of an enterprise activity to the local community.

   We made it relevant by involving pupils who adopted key roles in the organisation and development of the idea. We were assisted by our Foreign Language Assistant.

   The DVD was aimed at the whole learning community where it could be used as a way of promoting foreign language learning within the school community.

2. **How we encouraged pupils to take *responsibility***
   Brainstorming session to produce and discuss ideas
   Pupils took decisions on content and relevancy to current classes within each year group.

   Pupils took tasks and scripts were developed, discussed and altered as needed. The group appointed the Foreign Language Assistant as sole Director and requested her input to ensure that the research for the news programme reflected real life and culture of that country and that all scripts were accurate.

3. **How we involved partners in learning – building *relationships***

External = Business / Community / Parents & Families
- Link School in country specific to language
- Business/Community link from that culture.

Internal = Other adults in school
- The drama department
- Language teachers
- Audio-visual technician who demonstrated to the group how to operate the video and recording equipment and who then led sessions for pupils to gain "hands-on" experience.

4. **How we *reflected* on its success – assessment**
- Learned to work as part of a team and to contribute more effectively
- Opportunity to develop skills and confidence
- Developed an appreciation of working to a tight time schedule to complete the task
- Improved speaking skills in modern language
- Developed understanding of another culture
- Gained an insight into career opportunities
- Experience of marketing and sales.

5. ***Review* – further ideas for development**
- Make a DVD involving other members of staff
- Make the DVD longer but accessible to the majority of English-speaking people
- A DVD suitable for Spanish/French/German/Italian speaking people coming here as tourists.

Brief description
We produced a DVD in Spanish to give our new link school in the town of Vila-Real, Spain a flavour of life at our school.

By doing so, it gave us an introduction to the next topic on the syllabus. The DVD is an important part of the link we are in the process of establishing.

"Enterprising" it!

1. **How we made learning *relevant* by putting into a *real context***
The audience was our new link school in Spain.

Performances took place during class-time. We decided on the location for filming to take place. Pupils who were part of the school show assisted with delivery and performance.

We rehearsed in class before filming. It was necessary to discuss the project with staff and technicians in order to determine what would and wouldn't work.

The language areas chosen fitted neatly with the Standard Grade Spanish course. We had to do research on our own to find expression and language which were suitable. The curriculum content was adapted and used to produce a DVD.

2. **How we encouraged pupils to take *responsibility***
Agreement was reached between the pupils on who would do what, where and when.

We approached the Principal Teachers and staff of other departments to seek their support. We helped one another with the language input and any techniques which would improve our performance. We became "critical friends" to one another.

Curricular Areas

3. How we involved partners in learning – building relationships
   External = Business/Community/Parents & Families
   - Local businesses involved in the tourist trade
   - DVD production businesses
   - Local community involvement in partner town links
   - Spanish residents to outline culture differences
   - The school newsletter informed parents of the project.

   Internal = Other adults in school
   - Seven school departments
   - S1, 2 and 3 Guidance Teams
   - Senior Management Team
   - School Technicians.

4. **How we *reflected* on its success – assessment**
   We concluded that the experience had been extremely worthwhile and that something similar should be done in the near future.

   It made us aware of the next topic in Standard Grade and that this was an effective way of learning.

   It boosted our self-confidence and made us determined to approach our next level of Spanish with renewed interest.

   It also showed us what could be achieved with a little hard work.

   When we looked back at what we had done, we discussed our own performances and how they could be improved, the input from the departments and what they might offer in the future and our plans for the second DVD. The DVD was shown to S1, 2 and 3 classes, the School Board and members of staff. Comments were taken on board.

5. Review – further ideas for development
   - The DVD will be sent to the major of Vila-Real, Manolo Vilanova, Instituto Francesc Tarrega and local ceramic businesses that have shown interest in accepting pupils from our school on work experience placements
   - On our visit to Vila-Real, interviews will be conducted and filmed featuring Spanish pupils, teachers, businessmen and politicians
   - Our next DVD will focus on our town. It will show our Spanish counterparts the attractions that await them.

Mathematics

Curricular Areas

Brief description

The aim of the lesson was for the pupils to produce a batch of truffles after covering the topic "ratio", which also incorporates "estimation". Given a recipe for 80 truffles pupils had to use their knowledge of ratio to work out the ingredients required for their batch of truffles.

"Enterprising" it!

1. **How we made learning *relevant* by putting into a *real context***

   Groups competed to make the best batch of 20 truffles which were judged on flavour, quality, appearance and size. They had to design a label to market their truffles.

   The context of the lesson was set as in a factory. Differences between school and working in a factory were discussed
   - consequences of legal requirements
   - the rules that would apply: hygiene, health and safety
   - quality control
   - market forces
   - competition among companies to produce a product that the public wants to buy.

2. **How we encouraged pupils to take *responsibility***
   - Since it was a competition teamwork was of paramount importance to ensure the final goal was reached.
   - Choice was given to groups to assign roles within the group.

   The importance of personal responsibility was stressed to ensure that each step of the instructions was completed in the time given.
   Pupils had to manage their time effectively.

   Strict guidelines and deadlines were adhered to in order to produce a quality product.

Curricular Areas

3. **How we involved partners in learning – building *relationships***

External = Business/Community/Parents & Families

- Visit to a local bakery
- Visit from a young entrepreneur who runs a successful national food company.

Internal = Other adults in school

- Cross-curricular links with Art and Design and Home Economics Departments.

4. **How we *reflected* on its success – assessment**

- Quality control of product - team assessment
- Peer and staff assessed each product and provided feedback
- Assessed the effectiveness of their learning 'Ratios'. Tested pre and post activity
- Assessed personal learning skills – co-operation, confidence, creativity.

5. ***Review* – further ideas for development**

- Extending to make lesson suitable for more able pupils
- Further links with local food manufacturers.
- Whole school "Giant Truffle!" Maths Challenge.

Brief description
Applying classroom learning in a real context by making links with Art and Home Economics. An exhibition (presentation of knowledge) of learning was organised and presented through activity stations.

"Enterprising" it!

1. **How we made learning *relevant* by putting into a *real context***
    Firstly, as a class we discussed the topic of ratios used in the real world and what they mean. Cross-curricular links were then set up with Art, Home Economics and Science. In these subjects the pupils spent time working with ratios within subject contexts and then produced a display of knowledge showing how ratios relate to everyday life.

    This display was presented to their class peers and other years to consolidate their learning.

    The learning was also made more relevant by having a ratio activities day where pupils solved ratio problems in teams while working on real-life problems → eg. dividing money in ratios, dividing liquid in ratios.

2. **How we encouraged pupils to take *responsibility***
    *   Pupils presented back to the class on cross-curricular work and devised questions for their peers
    *   Setting ground rules about working well in teams eg. dividing up tasks, co-operating, communicating. The pupils went round ratio activity stations in groups. This meant the pupils had to decide themselves how to approach the problems and how to best use their team.

Curricular Areas

3. How we involved partners in learning – building *relationships*

External = Pupils made contact with the following:

- The Construction Industry Training Board (CITB) who were willing to come in and discuss concepts, such as ratios, and show how they would be used in the workplace.

External = other adults in school

- Art, Home Economics and Science Departments were involved. Staff discussed ideas. The school's enterprise co-ordinator also had a direct input to ensure cross departmental communication.

4. How we *reflected* on its success – assessment

Pupils discussed how they had encountered the topic in a different way from normal ie.

1. Cross-curricular units
2. Teamwork activities
3. Pupil presentations and questions.

A questionnaire was issued which found that the pupils enjoyed the experience and gained transferable skills such as working in a team and presentation skills.

In future the focus might be on the role pupils played within their teams and also look at how pupils developed over time.

5. *Review* – further ideas for development

- Development of further cross-curricular links
- Allow pupils to acquire more experience in making presentations
- More group work so they understand the benefits of team working
- Make up a game on topic – for peers or younger pupils.

Brief description
Students applied their knowledge of percentage decreases to this marketing activity and presented their learning to their peers and other staff.

"Enterprising" it!

1. **How we made learning *relevant* by putting into a *real context***
   Students were asked how a sale could be promoted and what sort of percentage discounts are generally on offer in the retail sector.

   Having mastered the percentage reduction technique, pupils, in groups, "set-up" their own business which was promoting a January sale.

   Pupils, in teams of four, were given poster paper, luminous card and a number of *Argos* catalogues.

   They had to give their business a trading name and then show their customers how much each percentage discount would save them, using PowerPoint presentation or similar.

   Having presented their results to an audience of peers and other staff, a prize was offered for the best poster, the most original business concept and the accuracy of the discounts offered.

2. **How we encouraged pupils to take *responsibility***
   Pupils had autonomy over business type, business name, and what was sold. They also decided on the discounts to be offered on the items that they decided to sell in their store.

   They had to adopt roles and work together to produce results.

   They made a display of our work for other students to look at.

Curricular Areas

3. How we involved partners in learning – building *relationships*

External = Business/Community/Parents & Families

- Pupils examined marketing techniques used by businesses to promote themselves and discussed the importance of image and professionalism
- Sales Advisor – guest speaker.

Internal = Other adults in school

- Other members of staff judged the posters to highlight the work of the department.
- Prizes were presented at school assembly
- Extras points were given in "Pupil Challenge" awards.

4. How we *reflected* on its success – assessment

Peers and staff had the opportunity to comment on the business ideas during the presentation of ideas.

The teacher formally assessed student accuracy in percentage decrease by marking the work before it was displayed on the poster, ie. effectiveness of learning.

Pupils assessed the personal learning gained through participating in this approach by sharing it with mentors in personal learning plans.

5. *Review* – further ideas for development

- Make use of ICT next time to make the posters look even more professional and give the students the opportunity to make flyers or mailings to promote their businesses
- Link with a number local business partners
- Link with Business Studies Department to discover more about marketing and advertising strategies
- Examine notion of percentage profit and loss.

Brief description

Working with bank staff and senior pupils, junior pupils use games to develop their knowledge of financial education and basic Maths skills. As a result they design and produce a booklet that teaches basic maths skills to primary school pupils.

"Enterprising" it!

1. How we made learning *relevant* by putting into a *real context*

- The concepts used in the games, reflect real life scenarios and encourage pupils to appreciate the context for learning
- One period per week, pupils work with trained volunteers developing Maths skills through games
- In groups, pupils are challenged to design and develop a booklet to teach basic skills to primary school pupils.

Audience: younger pupils and parents.

2. How we encouraged pupils to take *responsibility*

Pupils work in pairs with a volunteer. Maths games are designed to improve basic numeracy skills.

They have to explain answers and record progress in a diary. Parents are asked to record information with their children regarding the application of their knowledge in everyday situations (ie. bank account, savings, part-time work earnings).

Curricular Areas

3.	**How we involved partners in learning – building *relationships***
	External - = Business / Community / Parents & Families
	- Members of staff from bank working as volunteers.
	- Scottish Centre for Financial Education (See Learning and Teaching

	Internal = Other adults in school
	- Learning Support Staff
	- S6 pupils who work as volunteers helping selected pupils with their basic numeracy skills as part of their certificated programme of Peer Tutoring.

4.	**How we *reflected* on its success – assessment**
	The learning process is evaluated in diaries at the end of each session.
	Each pupil is assigned a tutor to discuss the diary and its contents and decide on future needs.

	The development of their transferable skills are discussed and assessed.

5.	***Review* – further ideas for development**
	- Now in second year. Training of volunteers reviewed and updated. New games purchased and developed. New ideas to 'Present their Knowledge' to younger pupils ie. games, booklets, quizzes, etc

	- Continue liaison with local Bank: develop new ideas to extend involvement to other whole school activities.

© Enterprising Careers, University of Strathclyde, 2007.

Religious &
Moral Education

Curricular Areas

Addressing Human and Moral Issues

Brief description
We focused on the value of human life, the moral issues involved in decision-making and how we could best put this into a 'real' context for learning.

"Enterprising" it!

1. **How we made learning relevant by putting into a real context**
    We planned and staged a mock slave auction as part of a topic area.

    We discussed the value of human life and the moral issues involved – why is it unacceptable for one human being to own another?

    Via the Internet, pupils researched modern slavery.

    We considered the ethical position of buying merchandise sold in the high street that could have been made by "slaves" in the Developing World. Should such goods be boycotted?

    The class ran their own 'slave market'.

    Audience: invited peer groups to come to the event.

2. **How we encouraged pupils to take *responsibility***
    They made placards to hang round the necks of 'slaves', on which they advertised skills, qualities, and present state of health. They tried to put an approximate cost on each. Would someone pay more for a highly skilled slave who had a track record of running away? . . . Or a talented slave with an unhealthy record? We discussed why some slaves are more valued than others.

    Pupils invited others to attend to be 'buyers' at the auction. They were issued with 'money'. Pupils explained to audience how an auction works and what was expected of them. Pupils organised and took part in the event.

Curricular Areas

3. **How we involved partners in learning – building *relationships***
   External = Business/Community/Parents & Families
   - We made contact with charities via the Internet and found out how they try to stop modern day slavery
   - We learned how widespread the problem was and invited one charity to the school to highlight its work
   - A local auctioneer.

   Internal = Other adults in school
   - All members of staff received invitations to the auction.

4. **How we *reflected* on its success – assessment**
   The class felt that they had learned a lot eg. more understanding of moral issues surrounding slavery today; how an auction works; more depth of understanding of value of human life – which was beyond price.

   They worked well as a team, enjoyed 'hosting' the event and they gained knowledge, confidence and enjoyment from the activity. This learning was assessed and recorded.

5. ***Review* – further ideas for development**
   - Pupils could do further work on slavery within other subject areas eg. Modern Studies and Geography
   - They could find out more about "Fairtrade" products
   - They could visit an auction and see how a real one worked.

Brief description

The aim of the lesson was to help pupils appreciate and understand all the different 'creation stories'. The basic premise underlying this lesson was to help pupils realise we all have creative powers. Harnessing their own 'creativity' will help themselves to have a deeper affinity, understanding, and an appreciation of these 'creative stories', ie. application of understanding in a 'real context.

"Enterprising" it!

1. **How we made learning *relevant* by putting into a *real context***
    It is very difficult to get one's mind around how we got here and to understand how the world/beauty of nature came into being!

    How could God/gods/supreme powers create the universe? How can we as human beings be creative? Class came up with the idea of creating a song. They produced a CD.

    Audience: peer group, staff, primary pupils, parents.

2. **How we encouraged pupils to take *responsibility***
    To demonstrate 'creativity', the pupils completed the song with minimum teacher input.

    To determine the mood/tone of the song they chose everything from the key the song would be in to whether it would be a rap, or a 12 bar blues, to the rhythm.

    They wrote the lyrics for all the verses and the chorus.

    They recorded their songs onto a CD.

    They presented the songs to an invited audience.

Curricular Areas

3. **How we involved partners in learning – building *relationships***
External = Business / Community / Parents & Families
- We visited a professional recording studio with session musicians.
- We performed it in front of parents/community
- Created a CD.

Internal = Other adults in school
- With the help of a music therapist in the school, who also has expertise in recording music in his music recording studio, we created a CD of the song, with pupils performing their own creation.

---

4. **How we *reflected* on its success – assessment**
The CD of their 'creation song' – tangible product.

Also formative assessment of all pupils involvement throughout. How motivated they were, the level of their participation etc.

---

5. ***Review* – further ideas for development**
Time is a huge factor. We did not have nearly as much time as we would have liked to record the song. We need to look at ways to develop this in future.
- To perform it to rest of school at assemblies
- To perform it at local radio station.

Brief description

A positive outcome of the course entitled "Justice in the World: Global Solidarity" was the establishment of a group who wished to raise awareness of world poverty and to raise enough money to build a school in a Third World country. Their first task was to introduce their vision to the whole school.

"Enterprising" it!

1. **How we made learning *relevant* by putting into a *real context***
   The audience was the whole school.

   We shared our knowledge and gave purpose to our learning through a PowerPoint presentation lasting 5 minutes which gave key facts about poverty and posed the question – *What Can We Do?*

   We used current images, statistics, and an inspiring piece of music to go alongside the presentation.

   As a result of this, we raised funds towards our campaign by running a series of of smaller monthly fund-raising activities.

2. **How we encouraged pupils to take responsibility**
   We met once a week, came up with ideas and agreed a plan of action for the forthcoming year.

   We took ownership by working independently during the school holidays to complete the presentation. When the presentation was being shown to the school during House Assemblies, we arrived at school shortly after 8am each morning!

   We co-operated with members of staff and with the Headteacher who, together with the Senior Management Team, was kept informed of progress.

   Our aim was to enthuse fellow pupils into sharing our vision.

   The pupils consistently worked together.

   A' Masked Dance' has been organised by the group which will take place in the coming weeks. Budgeting and enterprise skills have been employed.

Curricular Areas

3. **How we involved partners in learning – building *relationships***
External =
- SCIAF, World Health Organisation.

Internal = Other adults in school
- Good working relationships were established between pupils and staff
- Members of the Technical Support staff with whom they worked closely to ensure that smooth-running of their presentation.

4. **How we *reflected* on its success – assessment**
The assessment of the whole school presentation was marked by the encouragement and support given to the cause by staff and pupils in the form of cash donations and words of support.

The organising group has also benefited from their experiences, gaining a multitude of transferable skills such as in problem-solving self-evaluation, motivating others, working together, flexibility and creativity.

5. ***Review* – further ideas for development**
Our presentation was only the start. Many ideas for future fundraising are emerging

Two pupils were so inspired that they independently organised a sponsored cycle race, raising over £300.00.

© Enterprising Careers, University of Strathclyde, 2007.

Curricular Areas

Religious Observance Conference

Brief description
Religious Observance Conference: students planned, organised and participating in this half-day conference and delivered to an audience of peers.

"Enterprising" it!

1. **How we made learning *relevant* by putting into a *real context***
   - Using their knowledge of a variety of religions, senior pupils planned and delivered a conference to an audience
   - Organising workshops which enabled pupils to lead discussions in directions they wanted to learn about
   - Facilitating workshops, led by a variety of people with different belief systems.

2. **How we encouraged pupils to take *responsibility***
   Pupils were responsible for:
   - Considering issues in their own lives and how they affect lifestyle.
   - Planning and organising conference and workshops
   - Assuming roles/groups to take ideas forward
   - Discussing with external partners, input at conference
   - Outlining their own/group roles to act as facilitators or hosts at the event.

Curricular Areas

3. **How we involved partners in learning – building** *relationships*
    External = Pupils made contact with the following:
    *   Church Clergy (Christian)
    *   Muslim Leaders
    *   Humanists
    *   Youth Workers
    *   Scripture Union.

    Internal = Other adults in school
    *   RME Department
    *   Youth Workers.

4. **How we** *reflected* **on its success – assessment**
    *   Pupils completed self-evaluation sheets at the end of each workshop to identify their learning
    *   Plenary at end: discussed differences and similarities between different viewpoints, group assessment
    *   Exploration of how differences add to society and how tolerance and understanding helps us to deal with life issues
    *   Pupils assessed their personal learning through organisational skills, communication skills, self-awareness and awareness of others.

5. *Review* **– further ideas for development**
    *   Plans for next year include a full day conference to enable more workshops and greater choice, a larger audience and peers, various ages groups, parents and the wider community.

Science

- **Biology**
- **Chemistry**
- **Environmental**
- **Physics**

Brief description

S1 class worked in teams to produce a collaborative display of *Materials of the Earth*.

Teams demonstrated to their peers an experiment which demonstrated one property of a material.

"Enterprising" it!

1. **How we made learning *relevant* by putting into a *real context***
   Audience
   Peers in class, Science teaching staff
   Action – Task 1
   Pupils worked in teams to produce an informative display on a variety of topics – rocks, metals, oil, water, recycling, air pollution. Teams shared their knowledge of their chosen topic by presenting their findings to others.
   Action – Task 2
   As pupils gained confidence and skills working with others, the second task was to present an experiment which demonstrated a material's strength, flexibility, hardness, electrical conductivity, thermal conductivity or wear resistance. Relevance of the use of different materials and their properties in everyday life and the importance of conserving natural resources was explored.
   This activity was demonstrated to other pupils.

2. **How we encouraged pupils to take *responsibility***
   In order to achieve both tasks, the pupils took responsibility for:

   - deciding on roles for class members such as timekeeper, materials manager, facilitator and recorder of information
   - working together to use the resources available to produce a "display of knowledge"
   - developing a practical presentation following set criteria.

Curricular Areas

3. **How we involved partners in learning – building *relationships***

External = Business/Community/Parents & Families

- P7 Parents' Evening - collaborative display of all posters on corridor wall to show examples of S1 work in science
- Business applications from Science experts providing information
- ECO Schools Liaison Officer: recycling and other environmental issues.

Internal = Other adults in school

- Pupils presented quality posters and practical experiments to their peers and other science teaching staff on their research topic.

4. **How we *reflected* on its success – assessment**

Task 1 – Posters

Peer assessment with feedback and response.

Task 2 – Practical Presentations

The group carried out self-assessment of their performance against the set criteria and assessed their personal development skills eg. effective communication, problem-solving and creativity.

5. ***Review* – further ideas for development**

- Areas of weakness in the products or process were identified and are being used as targets for improvement in future collaborative learning tasks
- Providing demonstrations/presentations at Parents' Evenings
- Introducing Primary 7 pupils to the science curriculum at induction events.

Brief description
Pupils learning about what scientists do – biologists in particular - and what it might be like working a real-life situation. What were the key issues? What could be learned from real scientists that might be useful in school?

"Enterprising" it!

1. **How we made learning *relevant* by putting into a *real context***

   This speaks for itself – at times pupils do not see the relevance of a subject at school. A visit to a marine laboratory allowed pupils to see, at first-hand, scientists in the work place. They had the opportunity to talk with and ask questions of the scientists. As a result, the pupils compiled a report on their learning which was sent out as a newsletter and posted on the school website.

   Pupils set up the visit themselves and decided on the focus for discussion. This formed the basis for their 3 hour visit.

   - They arranged content, times and transport
   - The visit to a marine laboratory gave pupils the opportunity to watch scientists at work; asking questions about the practical application of Biology in the work place
   - Telephone calls, e-mails, discussion on content
   - A newsletter report then went to **all** parents.

2. **How we encouraged pupils to take *responsibility***

   In the course of an open discussion about why we teach pupils science at school and what sort of hands-on practical work they had done, pupils were asked if they had ever seen scientists at work or if they knew anyone who was a scientist. They then played a key role by writing to several laboratories stating why they would like to visit. They chose the best one and e-mail contact began. Pupils made decisions and took responsibility for initiating this business link.

   They planned and organised the visit
   They wrote letters of thanks
   They set up photographic displays and follow-ups.
   Finally they wrote a report about their experience.

Curricular Areas

3. How we involved partners in learning – building *relationships*

External = Business / Community / Parents & Families

- Parents
- Marine Laboratory staff.

Internal = Other adults in school

- Science Technicians and other department staff
- Senior Management Team members and the Careers Adviser.

4. How we *reflected* on its success – assessment

The group reflected upon their learning experience after the visit and summarised this on the whiteboard. At least one pupil was inspired to consider a career as a scientist. All realised that they had the capacity to link with people and groups outwith school and beyond the classroom. They could make this happen.

Discussion ensued about students having the power to create their own opportunities and to learn more in real life situations about the work that people do.

Skills development = responsibility for learning, effective communication, gathering and analysing information and working with others.

5. *Review* – further ideas for development

- Stimulating other teachers to think of such activities in their own teaching
- Bringing the "world of work" into the classroom more often
- Further trips to other 'scientists' at work
- Sharing the experience with others eg. Assemblies, Parents' Evenings
- Applied science links to be explored – medicine/hospital.
- Parents with careers in science: explore possibilites.

Curricular Areas

Business and the Curriculum

Brief description
The teaching objectives were achieved by using this enterprise activity approach, thus bringing the curriculum to life. We decided as a class to use the knowledge gained through the subject in a real situation.

"Enterprising" it!

1. **How we made learning *relevant* by putting into a *real context***
   - Pupils discussed the learning objectives associated with the topic of growing plants and how these could be transferred to a real context
   - Group discussion took place to ascertain the best source of plant materials ie. – those which would be attractive and marketable
   - All stages of the growing process were carried out as per learning objectives. Plants were 'priced out' and 'potted on'. Cuttings were taken as per business model in order to sell or to make school environment more appealing.

   Audience: community.

2. **How we encouraged pupils to take *responsibility***
   - A Business Plan was drawn up by pupils
   - Pupils priced goods to ensure a profit was made
   - Pupils organised themselves to take on specific tasks and then chose roles
   - Pupils managed the venture (watering plants, setting up tables, selling plants)
   - Pupils ordered and wrapped plants in attractive packaging for sale at Parents' Evening (at date closest to Mothers' Day). They also made instruction cards for care of plants
   - Pupils counted and audited money made at sales and planned how best to use the profit
   - Pupils decided to give a proportion of money made to charity and kept some aside to buy more resources (seeds, bulbs, compost) for the following year.

3. **How we involved partners in learning – building *relationships***
   External = Business/Community/Parents & Families
   - Local College Horticulture Department and Garden Centre personnel were guest speakers
   - Money made from plant sales was used to fund a day out for pupils to a local business which was renowned for its attractive floral displays
   - The courtyard outside the school office was tidied and plants placed in planters. Local businesses sponsored this
   - Parents purchased plants after receiving letters about the sale.

   Internal = Other adults in school
   - Another teacher played a key role in advising pupils on the care of plants.
   - Several members of staff (both teaching and non-teaching) participated in helping with the plant sales.

4. **How we *reflected* on its success – assessment**
   - Successful business –profit was secured to fund a successful and motivational trip for pupils involved in this activity. Pupils themselves decided on venue and format of day
   - Learning was more effective as pupils had to transfer their knowledge into a real experience for which they took full responsibility
   - Pupils reflected on their personal learning by completing evaluation forms and sharing these with mentors in Personal Learning Plans.

5. ***Review* – further ideas for development**
   - The success of the project has encouraged the department to repeat it
   - After summer, we plan to plant hyacinth bulbs for sale at Christmas and involve another year group thus extending the interest and pass on learning from the original project group to a new cohort.

Curricular Areas

© Enterprising Careers, University of Strathclyde, 2007.

Brief description
Investigating the use of micro-organisms in the production of yogurt as a food source and as a means of preserving milk. Applying this knowledge to assist others in Third World countries.

"Enterprising" it!

1. **How we made learning *relevant* by putting into a *real context***

   We discussed the advantages of yoghurt as a means of preserving milk and providing an alternative optional solid food source. We looked at the advantages of yoghurt production from goats milk in Third World countries. We also looked at "Kids for Bids" project, SCIAF and Fairtrade work which aim to enable families to sustain small industries and enterprise by ensuring a fair price for produce and to help provide the means to set up small industries. We decided to raise money to sponsor a small family-run yogurt making business in the Third World.

   Over a period of four weeks money was raised and sent to charity for use in small industries projects.

   Audience: Local and international communities.

2. **How we encouraged pupils to take *responsibility***
   - Pupils thought about how they could raise money
   - They decided to sell Fairtrade chocolate bars in school and Fairtrade yoghurt covered raisins
   - They linked this with the "Make Poverty History" campaign and "Comic Relief"
   - On "Red Nose Day", pupils organised a presentation and displayed information in and around the school.

   Fairtrade tea and coffee were provided from funds to introduce Fairtrade products into the staff room. The sale of chocolate bars was extended to the staff room.

   Pupils designed and displayed information about Fairtrade and small industries.

Curricular Areas

3. **How we involved partners in learning – building *relationships***
External = Business / Community / Parents & Families
- Local Co-op and Oxfam shops were involved as guest speakers. They also provided Fairtrade products for the school. Many pupils bought special Fairtrade chocolates for Mothers' Day gifts
- Parents.

Internal = Other adults in school
- All members of Biology Department
- Janitors and Technicians who helped in the organising of a whole school event day
- Catering staff and school staff introduced to use of Fairtrade products.

4. **How we *reflected* on its success – assessment**

All Biology students were involved and 4th year Biotechnology students were able to explain to other pupils and staff why they had chosen this activity.

A small class project expanded into a whole school activity
Links were established between: class Subjects/Comic Relief/Make Poverty History/SCIAF/Co-op/Oxfam/Fairtrade. Pupils are enthusiastic about repeating this next year.

Pupils reflected on their personal learning through working with such groups.

5. ***Review* – further ideas for development**
The Co-op have volunteered to provide a more in-depth presentation of Fairtrade products.

Pupils to approach catering staff to investigate the possibility of Fairtrade products in Dining Hall.

Repeat next year and possibly extend the range of Fairtrade products.

Pupils to look at sponsoring other projects through similar activities which link with other curricular areas.

Brief description
In groups, pupils researched details on principles, advantages and disadvantages of one type of Power Station.
The groups then reported back to the class through presentations. A debate followed as to the best option for sustaining our country's energy needs.

"Enterprising" it!

1. **How we made learning *relevant* by putting into a *real context***
    Instead of teaching the topic, the pupils were put into a real situation as consumers and asked about their present knowledge, the importance of energy on their lives, how they would find out about it, how they could inform others to enable them to decide on best sources of energy. Specific questions for this subject were:
    *   What would happen if you couldn't switch the lights on?
    *   What would it mean for *you*, your community, the country as a whole?
    *   Why do we need electricity? What do we use it for?
    *   How much do we need?
    *   What effect do Power Stations have on the environment/the economy/society?
    *   How can we best sustain our energy needs in future?
    *   If you were in government what decisions would *you* make to ensure sustainability?

2. **How we encouraged pupils to take *responsibility***
    *   They work in teams to complete task
    *   They organise themselves and delegate tasks and responsibilities eg research duties, technical details, poster design, art work – presentation to class
    *   Pupils work to deadlines
    *   Pupils have responsibility for content and quality of presentations
    *   Pupils listen to and respect different views and opinions
    *   They come to informed decisions based on research evidence.

Curricular Areas

3. How we involved partners in learning – building *relationships*

External = Business / Community / Parents & Families

Links were made with local projects

- Proposed wind farm development
- Hydro-electric Power Station.

Internal = Other adults in school

- Pupils interviewed other staff members re their views, clipboard in hand
- They also sought out some 'expert' advice from teachers in Geography, Biology and Physics Departments.

---

4. How we *reflected* on its success – assessment

Ongoing formative assessment, peer group evaluation

- brainstorming
- research
- distillation of ideas/edifying
- qualifying criteria for presentation agreed at start

ie.

- informative
- principles
- outlined/energy changes
- advantages/disadvantages
- good visual presentation
- final class vote
- review of personal qualities developed ie. level of responsibility, effective communication, co-operation and working with others.

---

5. *Review* – further ideas for development

- This group of subjects /topic could be developed as a cross-cutting theme within 'A Curriculum for Excellence' involving several departments. eg. Science, Geography, Modern Studies, Technology, Business Studies, Mathmatics
- Site visits to wind farms/Power Stations
- Seek the views of local/national politicians and councillors
- Research energy providers and cost to consumers.

Social Studies

- **History**
- **Geography**
- **Modern Studies**
- **Business Education**

Brief description
Pupils took part in a workshop, run by guest speakers from the local Fairtrade shop, with games and role play all designed to raise awareness of fair trade issues. At the end of the workshop the pupils were challenged to run a whole school awareness activity. This linked well with coursework "Trade and Aid" Unit.

"Enterprising" it!

1. **How we made learning *relevant* by putting into a *real context***
    A guest speaker who ran a Fairtrade shop and had visited workers in Third World countries invited the class to the shop and gave a presentation. He challenged the pupils to raise the profile of Fairtrade in the school.

    As a result, pupils raised awareness by:
    *   presenting at Assemblies
    *   writing articles for the school newsletter
    *   by selling Fairtrade goods at the tuck shop.

2. **How we encouraged pupils to take *responsibility***
    By challenging pupils to run an activity which would raise the profile of Fairtrade within the whole school, the pupils assumed responsibility by:
    *   devising a marketing strategy
    *   marketing the brand to the school as a whole
    *   planning and organising awareness-raising events
    *   working in teams and assuming roles within these
    *   managing themselves and their teams to complete the tasks.

Curricular Areas

3. **How we involved partners in learning – building *relationships***
   External = Business / Community / Parents & Families
   - Owner of a Fairtrade business came to give a presentation to pupils
   - Parent who had links with UNICEF spoke to class.

   Internal = Other adults in school
   - Home Economics Department helped pupils bake Fairtrade cakes
   - Other staff attended Fairtrade lunchtime activity.

4. **How we *reflected* on its success – assessment**
   Discussion with pupils afterwards reviewing what they learned and enjoyed.

   Questionnaires pre and post Fairtrade unit to measure understanding by others of Fairtrade.

   Assessment of personal learning gained and recorded by each pupil.

5. ***Review* – further ideas for development**
   - Could lead onto a group of pupils setting up a Fairtrade co-operative
   - Future links with UNICEF to link school with project in the Third World.

Brief description

This was a series of five lessons on Tropical Storms.

Pupils created a display of knowledge to present their knowledge and their understanding of the topic to an audience of peers, parents and primary pupils at an induction event.

"Enterprising" it!

---

1. **How we made learning *relevant* by putting into a *real context***
    Audience: The S1 classes, primary pupils, parents.
    Actions: Pupils were given a homework exercise asking them to think about:
    *   what they would like to find out about tropical storms and why it was important to know
    *   who could help
    *   where they could find information
    *   how they could present it to inform others.

    Following suggestions from pupils, pupils worked in groups and used ICT around a web page, school library, books to present information using a display of knowledge.

    To present to the class, and to others as a follow-up.

    Relevance: Pupils were developing transferable skills relevant to employment: working in groups, developing ICT skills, showing creativity, making presentations, finding information.

    Where possible, an example was made of the 2005 tropical storm, Hurricane Katrina, of which most pupils had some knowledge.

---

2. **How we encouraged pupils to take *responsibility***
    Outcomes: The class discussed the homework exercise making suggestions, then planned how to achieve learning objectives in groups.

    While in groups, some teaching and learning was facilitated by the teacher through formative discussion and targeted question & answer sessions, but pupils had access to library information booklets and Internet reducing the amount of teacher reliance and increasing pupil responsibility.

    Pupils worked independently on computers linked to a BBC web page on Hurricane Katrina.

    Pupils co-operated and decided which part they would each take in order to achieve outcomes and complete task.

    Relevance: As stated, Hurricane Katrina was referred to frequently. Links to work and employment were also made.

© Enterprising Careers, University of Strathclyde, 2007.

Curricular Areas

3. **How we involved partners in learning – building *relationships***
   External = Pupils made contact with the following
   - Weather Reporter
   - Travel Adviser

   Internal = other adults in school
   - Librarian
   - ICT Department

4. **How we *reflected* on its success – assessment**
   Both pupils and the teacher were assessed at the end of this scheme of work through a simple questionnaire:
   - How much did you enjoy geography this week? (Scale of 1-5)
   - Tick the transferable skills you used this week. (Selected skills listed)
   - If you worked in a group, what was your job?
   - How did you get your job?
   - Were you happy about the job you did?
   - Why do you feel like this?
   - If you could change how you worked this week, what would you change?

   Teacher assessment:
   - How well was the enterprise organised by the pupils?
   - Did everyone know the aims of the lessons? Was their knowledge and understanding consolidated?
   - How well did the pupils work together?
   - Did all pupils fulfil their roles within the project? How could these be developed next time?
   - Were resources used and applied well?
   - How did pupils receive feedback about the success of their enterprise?
   - Was it a positive, rewarding and enjoyable experience? How do your know?
   - Next time, what would you change and why?

   Achievement:
   The class discussed how pupils might be assessed. This was largely based around the learning objectives. The teacher faciliated discussion about assessing transferable skills and improvements to work practice.

5. ***Review* – further ideas for development**
   Present to another class and to whole year groups
   Pupils should become increasingly familiar with working in groups.
   Improving links with external partners eg. MET office personnel to assess, content and talk about career pathways.

Curricular Areas

Brief description
Democracy Unit. Class chose to be in one of 4/5 political parties or in media group.

A political campaign run by various parties with the media group reporting on events.

"Enterprising" it!

1.   How we made learning *relevant* by putting into a *real context*

Pupils had knowledge of the processes of election campaigning and were simulating real life events.

Pupils learned by taking an active part in the campaign.
The 'competitive' nature of this activity ensured that pupils took ownership and were motivated to do well.

Each party had to produce a poster, a leaflet, a rosette and a speech. The media group covered the campaign with newspaper articles, interviews, video recordings and photos.

S2 class spent 4-6 periods on this activity.

---

2.   How we encouraged pupils to take *responsibility*

Pupils were given a remit at the start. They selected which group they wished to work in and decided on roles.
The class attended the library/Internet room for one period during which time they did internet research.
Each group was responsible for deciding what it was going to do and what role each group member would play.
Pupils took responsibility for planning their input, carrying out their task and participating in the campaign event.

---

3. **How we involved partners in learning – building *relationships***
   External = Business/Community/Parents & Families
   - This activity was preceded by a visit to the school by the local MSP who spoke to pupils about her job and about election campaigns.

   Internal = Other adults in school
   - Cross-curricular work with teacher of Media Studies. The media group received instruction from the Technician before using the digital camera and video recorder.

4. **How we *reflected* on its success – assessment**
   Activity was assessed in a 'formative' way as opposed to summative assessment. Comments and feedback were given by the teacher on each group's work.

   Pupils were encouraged to self-evaluate afterwards – how this approach impacted on their learning.

   Pupils evaluated the impact on their personal learning – self-awareness, working with others, co-operation, planning and organisation.

5. ***Review* – further ideas for development**
   - Similar activities with other S2 classes, then with S3/4
   - Invite MSP and local councillors to the campaign event in order to provide feedback
   - Deliver campaign to other year groups and encourage them to sign up/elect a winner.

© Enterprising Careers, University of Strathclyde, 2007.

Brief description
To demonstrate real-life application of a Modern Studies topic.

Pupils worked with students from two neighbouring schools to stage a mini-trial which took place in the local Sheriff Court. This allowed them to gain an awareness of the various roles within the judicial system in addition to honing their presentation and communication skills.

"Enterprising" it!

1. **How we made learning *relevant* by putting into a *real context***
   A mock trial was staged in a real life court room with pupils, parents and court officials as the audience/jury.

   Court officials visited the school to give pupils advice on procedure and this set the scene.

   Pupils acted out the roles of court officials such as Sheriff, Sheriff Clerk, Procurator Fiscal, Defence Lawyer and the accused.

   The relevance of what they had learned in the classroom became obvious. Pupils reflected on their learning by 'doing it'. That was by far the best part of the whole experience. By reconstructing the roles of the people involved in a criminal trial, the pupils became absorbed in their own particular role, allowing them to experience what it was like to be involved in the criminal justice system.

2. **How we encouraged pupils to take *responsibility***
   The pupils took ownership of the proceedings by choosing and preparing their roles prior to the court case. An area business manager who is responsible for liaising with schools and organising events worked with the young people and advised them on choosing their roles.

   Pupils were responsible for ensuring that everything was planned for the day.

   The pupils also spent several weeks organising and preparing for the various parts that they would be acting out in the court room.

   Certain pupils formed part of the jury, therefore the decision-making lay with them once the evidence had been presented.

Curricular Areas

3. How we involved partners in learning – building *relationships*

External = Business / Community / Parents & Families

- Representatives from the Crown Office, Procurator Fiscal Service, Victim Support, Victim Information Service and Witness Service gave an outline of their roles in the criminal justice system and answered questions from pupils
- Pupils were also able to speak with representatives from Reliance, the private sector firm which provides prisoner escort facilities
- A visit to the cells, an experience which they found quite daunting, was also part of the learning experience
- Teachers and pupils from other schools participated
- Parents were involved in assisting and participating.

Internal = Other adults in school

- English Department – Debating Club – skills/links for public speaking.

---

4. How we *reflected* on its success – assessment

Working with pupils from two other schools added to the experience. Pupils were able to develop their teamworking, public speaking and debating skills. Pupils found their experience enormously beneficial because it was a real-life situation which all of them had hitherto only seen on television. It allowed them to appreciate the importance of planning and preparation, which was critical before the trial, and also the attention to detail to ensure no mistakes were made.

They assessed their own learning experience.

The lesson highlighted how beneficial active participation is in the learning process. Not only did the learning come to life but there were so many different facets which allowed the pupils to gain a whole host of skills. In addition, they really enjoyed it.

---

5. *Review* – further ideas for development

- Annual event
- Modern Studies Department display/re-enactment/film
- Local press – photo opportunities.

Curricular Areas

New business opportunity

Brief description
Pupils are required to choose a suitable location for a children's play centre, to be operated by a leading supermarket chain.

"Enterprising" it!

1. **How we made learning *relevant* by putting into a *real context***
   Pupils viewed a DVD of a Real Life business set-up involving a play centre - Flying Fortress from TV series "Risking It All". They learned of the difficulties faced prior to and during the business start-up. Discussion focused on key issues and how they might be resolved.

   Pupils were charged with setting up a children's play centre on one of the 3 potential sites. They worked in association with the local Business Park Manager.

   Issues such as pollution, noise, environmental concerns, availability of a labour force, infrastructure and potential markets were addressed.

   The task was to prepare a PowerPoint presentation demonstrating their research findings and justifying their decision.

   Audience:
   This was presented to, and assessed by the Business Forum in the town.

2. **How we encouraged pupils to take *responsibility***
   Each pupil took responsibility for the project research, using the Internet to find out about similar existing businesses, availability of appropriate equipment and health and safety legislation.

   They worked in groups to discuss, analyse and provide a solution.

   This was delivered in the form of a presentation to a business audience.

   Pupils participated to the full, taking on roles and responsibilities and all accepting new challenges.

Curricular Areas

3. **How we involved partners in learning – building *relationships***
   External = Business/Community/Parents & Families
   - Parents/families: pupils developed a questionnaire and were encouraged to discuss with their parents whether they would use such a facility. They involved them in the selection of a preferred site
   - Business links: discussions with businesses who have set up similar projects
   - Local Council Planning Department: presentation on points to be considered
   - Local community invited to attend.

   Internal = Other adults in school
   - Staff in school: the views of teaching, catering, cleaning and janitorial staff were considered via a questionnaire.

4. **How we *reflected* on its success – assessment**
   As the teacher leading the challenge I reflected on its success by looking back on the enthusiasm with which pupils tackled the project, the high quality of presentations which they created and the effectiveness of the pupils' learning.

   Pupils reflected on their success by having the opportunity to discuss as a group what they had achieved as a result of the project.

   Evaluations showed that a number of skills had been developed: confidence, co-operation, creativity, gathering and analysing information.

5. ***Review* – further ideas for development**
   - Business sponsorship for future ventures
   - Regular contact with the new children's play centre
   - Preparation of a school staff questionnaire/parents' questionnaire
   - Liaison with school work experience co-ordinator for the setting up of future placements.

Entrepreneurs of the future

Brief description
A project where pupils in groups created and launched a unique product. Each group had four weeks to think of a project, build a prototype and devise a marketing plan which included the sketch/storyboard for an advert and the aim was to consolidate their learning.

"Enterprising" it!

1. **How we made learning *relevant* by putting into a *real context***
   We had a discussion about new products on the market and what was unique about them. Pupils had a brainstorming session to devise ideas.

   In groups, pupils then focused on their own idea and promoted these ideas throughout the school. They also conducted market research.

   They devised a marketing strategy, and built their prototype. Pupils then contacted local businesses for inspiration and materials.

   Pupils presented their product, to a "panel" of educators and business people to gauge interest in potential development of the idea.

---

2. **How we encouraged pupils to take *responsibility***
   Pupils worked collaboratively taking roles, setting their own deadlines and combining resources.

   They communicated with one another in teams and with external partners.

   Pupils generated ideas and worked together to develop and build a prototype and marketing plan.

   They planned and organised a presentation for an audience.

---

3. How we involved partners in learning – building *relationships*

External = Business/Community/Parents & Families

- Business/Parents
- We asked local Young Enterprise Scotland Business Advisers to join the "panel" in order to judge the best product. They encouraged pupils to pursue their ideas
- Royal Bank of Scotland: Facing Up to Finance resource. Liaison with Royal Bank of Scotland.

Internal = Other adults in school

- Pupils contacted other teachers who could help with ICT, and final production.

4. How we *reflected* on its success – assessment

We reflected on what had been learned via formal assessment at the end of the topic as part of the curriculum in ICT.

Pupils, having made decisions based on research and collaboration with others, were able to review their successes and consider what they might have done differently.

Presentations offered both peers and the class teacher the opportunity to give feedback on the project and allow pupils to evaluate themselves, and others.

Pupils were encouraged to write about their experience stating what they had learned both in terms of skills and personal development.

5. *Review* – further ideas for development

- To make one of the products for development and testing on the open market, for example asking the school's Young Enterprise company to take the idea forward, develop it and sell it.

Curricular Areas

Brief description
Pupils were asked to design a board game to enhance their knowledge of the production process and to develop their knowledge of marketing.

"Enterprising" it!

1. **How we made learning *relevant* by putting into a *real context***
   Business Management classes (3) took part in this activity.

   We gave purpose to the learning through creating a "design and manufacturing process" activity which was to allow pupils to design a board game for their peer group. They also had to develop a marketing plan for the game.

   The audience was their peer group who would assess the product's effectiveness, suitability, design and quality.

2. **How we encouraged pupils to take *responsibility***
   In groups, pupils generated ideas by brainstorming.

   Decisions were made by the group and they took ownership by working as a team and contributing to the task.

   The pupils chose roles based on their skills eg. art work, design and presentation skills.

   They planned, co-ordinated and sourced their project to produce a functional board game.

   They planned and developed a presentation to their peers.

Curricular Areas

3. **How we involved partners in learning – building *relationships***
   External = Business / Community / Parents & Families
   - Manufacturer and designer of board games
   - Families: surveyed favourite board games.

   Internal = Other adults in school
   - Art & Design, Craft & Design Departments.

4. **How we *reflected* on its success – assessment**
   Product viability = Pupils reflected on the success by playing each game and making constructive comments regarding the worthiness of each.

   Quality = The design process and issues of quality were assessed. There was also discussion regarding the contribution of and individual strengths of team members.

   Subject knowledge and understanding= Effective learning assessed. Transferable skills assessed – achievement/confidence/working with others/me.

5. ***Review* – further ideas for development**
   - Next time pupils intend to award prizes for best ideas and publicise the venuture on the school website.

© Enterprising Careers, University of Strathclyde, 2007.

Brief description
In order to raise funds for a school trip, pupils set up and ran a business called "Scarves r us". Scarves were hand-knitted and sold to family, friends and staff.

"Enterprising" it!

1. **How we made learning *relevant* by putting into a *real context***

   The real purpose was that pupils needed to raise funds for a trip and to get started they had to agree a fund raising activity. Suggestions were made and discussed.

   The "best" project on which to embark was voted upon.

   Pupils were involved in learning about the running of a business, opening a bank account and keeping accounts.

   Roles were assumed such as Chairman, Management Team, Finance Team, Sales Team, Market Research Team.

2. **How we encouraged pupils to take *responsibility***

   The pupils organised all business meetings, deciding on an agenda and taking minutes. They learned to knit scarves.

   They opened a bank account with the school accountant and kept a note of money spent and brought in. Pupils understood that this was their small business and took ownership of it by making their own decisions.

   They carried out market research looking at comparable items and prices to raise their awareness of competitors' quality control. They interviewed members of the public to ascertain the demand for their product.

Curricular Areas

3. **How we involved partners in learning – building *relationships***
    External = Business / Community / Parents & Families
    - Business consultant – Prince's Trust – was involved to assist in business start-up skills
    - Wool and needles purchased locally – worked with local haberdashery
    - Asked for donation of wool from a Residential Centre for the Elderly, visited and made contact. Some residents helped with knitting skills.
    - Many parents supported by helping with knitting skills
    - Scarves sold within the community
    - Market research carried out
    - Contact with members of the public.

    Internal = Other adults in school
    - Worked closely with the school accountant.
    - Market research within the school.
    - Sales team sold to school staff and pupils

4. **How we *reflected* on its success – assessment**
    Practical assessment by looking at funds made and success in selling stock. Continual review as we adapted types of scarves, in accordance with customers' needs.

    Development of a new practical skill.

    Customer feedback was excellent and this inspired looking at product, pricing it and marketing it. Discussion took place with our business consultant as to where pupils could have developed marketing and production.

    Reflection on the skills pupils gained through running a business – self-awareness, working together and confidence.

5. ***Review* – further ideas for development**
    Pupils applied for a grant to buy a knitting machine and wool and they will continue their business by knitting "beanies" (hats).

    Expansion of market is being looked into. A business consultant for the Prince's Trust is working with the pupils to aid future motivation.

Brief description
Pupils formed a "publishing company" within the classroom. They made use of reprographic equipment and software to create comb-bound booklets on a revision topic of their choice.

"Enterprising" it!

1. **How we made learning *relevant* by putting into a *real context***
    Pupils in Administration are taught about reprographics equipment and software. We decided to bring this topic to life by arranging for pupils to use the equipment and software to create a booklet on a revision topic.

    This project had the added advantage of revising a previous topic.

    It was decided that the booklet should:
    *   have front and back covers which were laminated
    *   be bound using the comb-binding machine
    *   have at least one page which was created with desktop publishing software
    *   have a least one picture which they had taken using a digital camera
    *   have at least one page which had been printed using the colour printer.

    Topics possible were:
    *   workplace layout, health & safety, reception & security, mail handling or reprographics.

    Audience – peers, younger pupils, parents.

2. How we encouraged pupils to take *responsibility*

Pupils were given responsibility for:

- decision-making related to the task
- finding information for the booklet
- co-operating with their group members, assigning roles and responsibilities
- taking photos both within and outwith the classroom
- using equipment in a responsible and mature manner
- planning and organising the task.

In groups, they had to choose:

- a name for their publishing company
- a topic for their booklet
- who was going to do each task
- where they would get the information required for the booklet
- what pictures they were going to take.

3. How we involved partners in learning – building *relationships*

External = Business/Community/Parents & Families

- Bookbinder/printer to discuss production process, costs, etc.
- Careers in publishing: Careers Scotland Adviser
- BBC Bitesize Revision Aids.

Internal = Other adults in school

- Pupils went out and about around the school taking photos. They liaised with office staff to pose for reception photos and janitorial staff to pose as security guards. The community policeman also had his photo taken for the security topic.

4. How we *reflected* on its success – assessment

Pupils were asked to fill in an evaluation form which focused on:

- the aspects of the project they had enjoyed most eg. using the machinery, designing the booklet and taking the photos.
- reflecting on their experience of working as a team
- their opinion of active learning compared to other methods. The topic was then briefly reassessed to establish that pupils had gained a greater understanding of the reprographics topic. Personal transferable skills development was assessed – creativity, working with others, communication and confidence.

5. *Review* – further ideas for development

- This project has now been embedded as part of the Administration course. Future topics will now be developed in a similar way.

Curricular Areas

Brief description

The class purchased pens with the school name printed on them and sold them to friends and family. They recorded income and expenditure and drew up final accounts. The purpose was to consolidate learning.

"Enterprising" it!

1. **How we made learning *relevant* by putting into a *real context***

   Accounting pupils are taught how to record money going into and out of a business. It was decided to bring this to life by selling a real product and recording the receipt of real money.

   The profit was distributed to charity.

   The *class* was asked to:
   - decide on a name for the company
   - open accounts showing the purchase of the pens
   - open accounts to show the money received for pens
   - open expense accounts
   - calculate the profit or loss
   - compile a balance sheet
   - decide on a charity to donate the profits to.

2. **How we encouraged pupils to take *responsibility***
    Each *group* took responsibility for:
    - Forming a sales team
    - Deciding on a name for the sales team
    - Deciding on a strategy for selling the pens
    - Keeping a record of sales to identify the best sales team.

3. **How we involved partners in learning – building *relationships***
    External = Business/Community/Parents & Families
    - Parents and families were involved in purchasing the products
    - The profit was distributed to a local charity
    - Business adviser talks on suppliers, sales, and recording-keeping, etc.
    - University Business Department: careers in marketing/business/related work experience.

    Internal = Other adults in school
    - The school provided the initial capital from the School Management Team to buy the pens, which was then repaid
    - Staff in the school also purchased pens either for themselves or as class prizes.

4. **How we *reflected* on its success – assessment**
    Pupils were asked to complete an evaluation form at the end of the series of Subjects.

    Self-assessment focused on:
    - Enjoyment of the project
    - Skills learned from the project
    - Their role in the team.

    Teacher assessment focused on:
    Marks in later tests to assess improved understanding of recording transactions.

    Feedback from pupils was very positive and their learning was enhanced.
    Assessment marks showed an improved understanding of the topic.

5. ***Review* – further ideas for development**
    - This project has been incorporated into our courses on a permanent basis and has improved pupil motivation.

Technologies

- **Craft & Design**
- **ICT**
- **Technical**

Brief description
A group of pupils, based in the Technical Department, advertise for commissions/projects through the school. They then research the project, produce and sell the items requested. This allows us to put their learning into a real context, whilst motivating and engaging the pupils.

"Enterprising" it!

1. **How we made learning *relevant* by putting into a *real context***
   The skills learned in the subject are applied in a real situation as the pupils design and make products on request.

   The pupils used the school noticeboards as a medium to ask for design briefs from any department in the school.

   To date, the pupils have made a table for the Rector's office, easels for the Art Department, a bookcase for the Geography Department and picnic tables for the school grounds. They have also made a picnic table for a Social Work project.

   The pupils order the materials, price the project and share any profits made in the sale.

2. **How we encouraged pupils to take *responsibility***
   The pupils are given responsibility for:
   - seeking commissions
   - pricing materials
   - ordering materials
   - negotiating a price
   - making the item to specified quality level
   - agreeing on the division of profits.

3. **How we involved partners in learning – building *relationships***
   External = Business/Community/Parents & Families
   - Business: advice from businesses supplying similar products to the public
   - Suppliers: Pupils contacted suppliers for materials and negotiated prices
   - Community project: aimed at helping vulnerable young people.

   Internal = Other adults in school
   The pupils, most of whom displayed "challenging" behaviour, have negotiated with Heads of Departments at each stage of each project.

4. **How we *reflected* on its success – assessment**
   - The pupils involved in *Enterprise through Craft* all had a high exclusion rate from school, but behaviour was much improved in this class. Their products were well received
   - Each pupil had a sizeable cash payout at the end of the year as a result of their success
   - Their learning was purposeful and effective
   - They assessed their skills development
   - Pupils assessed their personal learning – confidence, creativity, team work and communication.

5. ***Review* – further ideas for development**
   In addition to tackling projects generated within the school, the group are going to produce a standard item, possibly clocks. These can be made during 'less busy' times and sold at Craft Fairs.

Curricular Areas

Brief description
Design, manufacture, marketing and gaining funding for a new product.

"Enterprising" it!

1. **How we made learning *relevant* by putting into a *real context***
   Pupils are introduced to the concept of enterprise through a presentation and series of activities including developing a prototype, manufacturing a product, securing funding, presenting ideas and marketing with a local business person.

   The focus is on creating a product and starting up a business. Information is given by a bank manager on the funding process. Prototype designers advise as to the stages involved in creating a new product.

   Each group is given a "Pringles" tube from which they have to develop a product.

   The pupils have to develop an idea, produce a prototype of it, prepare marketing information and prepare a Business Plan.

   A presentation is given to the team of business experts/financial advisers who are the "lenders".

   A decision is then taken as to whether the financial advisers will lend the funds required for the business start-up for the Pringles tube idea.

---

2. **How we encouraged pupils to take *responsibility***
   Each group is responsible for:
   - making all decisions
   - working as a team
   - deciding on roles
   - creating a product
   - working co-operatively to complete the project on time.

3. **How we involved partners in learning – building *relationships***
External = Business/Community/Parents & Families
- The introductory lesson is delivered by a local businessperson
- Careers Scotland Enterprise in Education Adviser
- Careers Scotland provided certificates for each pupil.
- Bank Manager
- Entrepreneur
- Product Designers
- Marketing Managers
- Parents: marketing appeal.

Internal = Other adults in school
- During the production stage some groups enlisted the help of other departments in the school – eg Art, Design & Technology and Business Studies Dept.

4. **How we *reflected* on its success – assessment**
- Pupils present their business idea to the funders, and received feedback/evaluation
- As well as examining finance, the feedback given also focuses on the development of enterprise skills, problem-solving skills, the ability to work as a team and business knowledge
- Pupils evaluate the success of the enterprise activity as a group
- Pupils assess their learning about business acumen
- Pupils assess their personal strengths– confidence, creativity, working together and problem-solving

5. *Review* **– further ideas for development**
- This course now takes place every year and is continually developed and refined. In the next session, it is hoped to work more closely with Careers Scotland
- The 'real' context could be developed by creating a sustainable, useful, marketable product within the class for sale to pupils/staff/parents/ community at a school event.
- By not limiting product development to a particular item (ie. Pringle Tube) but allowing more creative thought into producing something of value now that the process of developing and marketing has been tried and tested.

Brief description

This topic had been developed in recent years following a visit to a University Product Design Department to gain an insight into rapid Prototyping and to Product Design within a commercial content.

"Enterprising" it!

1. **How we made learning *relevant* by putting into a *real context***
   Students were able to consolidate their learning and provide solutions for their assignments by visiting a department at the university. Students are required to place their final projects in a commercial context.

   Seeing facilities and meeting practitioners who operate commercially enhanced pupil learning.

   The relevance of learning was evident and enabled students to make links when producing assignment reports.

   Final projects were presented as part of a competition.

   Audience –staff as judges.

2. **How we encouraged pupils to take *responsibility***
   Pupils outlined their plans to the practitioners ie. with the university professionals. Students answered/asked questions in an unfamiliar setting.

   Students were able then to make direct correlations between their work and real world applications in their reports.

   This developed pupils' skills in communication, working with others, problem-solving, flexibility and creativity

Curricular Areas

3. **How we involved partners in learning – building *relationships***
   External - = Business / Community / Parents & Families
   - Relationship with university department established over several years.
   - University Schools Liaison Officer – visit to school.

   Internal = Other adults in school
   - Technicians and Art Department.

4. **How we *reflected* on its success – assessment**
   Discussion on links to curriculum. We assessed that effectiveness of learning by putting into real world context.

   Pupils could see the application of their learning.

   This liaison between school and university department has increased numbers of pupils opting for this particular degree course.

   Pupils also assessed their person learning achievements – working with others and communication

5. ***Review* – further ideas for development**
   - Increase the time spent within the university department. Introduce more "hands-on" activities.

Brief description

We developed a project entitled "Surfing Holiday". Pupils had to research the relevant details, and prepare a presentation to convince the Headteacher that this was a worthwhile trip for pupils. The project ran for 6 weeks and integrated many new ICT skills.

"Enterprising" it!

1. How we made learning *relevant* by putting into a *real context*

Pupils watched a short video about university students on a surfing trip, in order to stimulate ideas. A series of tasks were set where the skills required were taught but the context of the materials was of the pupils own choosing.

Pupils researched the best places to surf in the UK, the best times to surf, costs of accommodation, travel and equipment. These prices had to be calculated using information from both the web and suppliers.

Pupils then had to select the two best places for a surfing holiday and deliver their findings in a presentation to the class.

They produce a marketing leaflet to provide other pupils with information on this type of holiday.

2. How we encouraged pupils to take *responsibility*

Responsibility for research both in and out of the classroom was central to the project. Pupils put together a presentation to deliver to peers. Some pupils worked together to research the data while others worked independently. Deadlines were agreed and set.

Curricular Areas

3. **How we involved partners in learning – building *relationships***
   External = Business/Community/Parents & Families
   - Business. We encouraged pupils to contact businesses either by email or by telephone to acquire information on costs
   - Parents' views of their children taking part in surfing were analysed in evaluation forms.

   Internal = Other adults in school
   - The Business Studies Department helped with ideas and also became involved in the project.

---

4. **How we *reflected* on its success – assessment**
   We reflected on what had been learned by formal assessment at the end of the project

   Pupils made decisions based on research and collaboration working.

   Peers and the class teacher gave feedback on the project. Self-evaluation also took place.

   Pupils were encouraged to include a short piece on their learning experience which included how they had applied their knowledge in this real context and how their personal learning had developed – 'About Themselves'.

---

5. ***Review* – further ideas for development**
   - Liaison with the Modern Languages Department would increase cross-curricular contact, linking in with future trips they plan to organise
   - Make contact with a travel agent who could use the marketing leaflets or who would come to school to hear and advise on the presentations.

Curricular Areas

Marketing a Business

Brief description
Pupils were asked to produce promotional material for a new business through application of their ICT skills. Groups created a display of materials and made a presentation of their promotional ideas.

"Enterprising" it!

1. **How we made learning *relevant* by putting into a *real context***
   Pupils were to create a company, a logo and a marketing strategy.

   They looked at the importance of corporate logos and advertising slogans using examples from local businesses and from the Internet.

   They had to make it real by working together to create a display and plan a group presentation to the class, before presenting to a team of experts.

2. **How we encouraged pupils to take *responsibility***
   Pupils worked in groups to:
   - create a company name, logo and slogan
   - choose roles and responsibilities to achieve the tasks
   - produce promotional material for their company
   - design a presentation to promote their company's advertising campaign
   - deliver presentation to their peers
   - deliver presentation to group of marketing specialists.

Curricular Areas

3. **How we involved partners in learning – building *relationships***

   Extent = Business/Community/Parents & Families

   - Local businesses and colleges were contacted and asked to provide samples of their promotional material and products. Online examples of promotional activity were also used to illustrate the variety of ways that businesses let people know about their products
   - FE and local businesses judged the final presentations.

   Internal = Other adults in school

   - Members of the Senior Management Team were invited to observe the group presentations and select the best promotional campaign.

4. **How we *reflected* on its success – assessment**

   In class, we considered what we had learned about a business and the range of ICT skills that were needed to produce the promotional materials. All pupils made use of desktop publishing software for a real purpose – many for the first time – by exploring the templates and facilities that it offers. All pupils acknowledged the skills that they had acquired, and decision-making and team-building experiences.

5. ***Review* – further ideas for development**

   - We intend to introduce a more formal evaluation of learning
   - We will research commissions from local businesses.

Section 4

Toolkits

How to use Section 4 Toolkits

Pupils' learning can be reinforced by formative and summative assessment to help them to recognise what they have learned. Using an enterprising approach enables this to take place effectively.

This will involve putting in place certain strategies to ensure that the pupils are aware of how to assess their effectiveness, their achievements and their learning throughout their education.

This section provides a variety of templates which can be built into the process.

The assessment process should not be onerous and although the templates include several questions, only a few of answers should be requested at any one time. So for example 'All About My Learning' may involve the pupil addressing only questions 1 and 2 at the first stage of the enterprise process. Over time, as the answers accumulate, this method of recording the impact / benefits of enterprise will provide a more in-depth picture of personal learning.

Toolkits for pupils:

- *'About Me'* is a benchmarking activity to establish current levels of enterprising skills and attitudes.
- *'About Another Person'* builds upon the above, encouraging pupils to appreciate the skills of others
- *'About Working Together'* encourages the pupils to look at their ability to work with others
- *'All About My Learning'* lets pupils see how they are progressing their learning
- *'Reflecting on Personal Learning'* provides pupils with an understanding of their personal achievements and development
- *'My Job'* takes pupils through their roles in the enterprise planning
- *'How I Felt'* encourages them to think about their part in the process
- *'Using My Skills'* provides the pupils with an understanding of what they are good at.

Toolkits for teachers:

- *'Teacher Evaluation'* provides the teacher with an ongoing record of individual achievement
- *'How Enterprising Are You?'*
- *How to enterprise a lesson*
- *How to debrief effectively* – a teambuilding exercise example
- *How to audit* Enterprise Activity in Your School or Department

Toolkits

How Enterprising Are You?

Approach	Progressing from →	1	2	3	4	5	6	7	8	9	10	To being *More Enterprising*
Teaching	Content – Driven											Process – Driven
Methodology	Teacher - Led											Student – Directed
Teacher's Role	Expert											Facilitator
Pupil's Role	Passive											Eager
Pupil Involvement	Needs help											Can contribute
Place	Mainly Classroom											Wider community flexibility
Timetable	Set											Flexible
Working with Others	Haphazard											Planned
Ethos	My world											Shared world
Risk-Taking	To be avoided											To be learned from
Assessment	For formal reporting											For learning
Assessing	By teacher											By collaboration
Outcomes	Quick fix											Lifelong included
Use of adults other than teachers	Rarely included											Frequently included
Planning	Reactive											Proactive
Leadership	Autocractic											Democratic
Openness to challenge from learners	Not willing											Willing

This is adapted for Scottish purposes from "Enterprising Ways to Teach and Learn' Book 2 – *Paul Kearney*

About Me

Rating my level of enterprising skills and attitudes

I can do the following: Name: _____

	Low 1	2	3	4	High 5	In what way?
Take responsibility for myself/task	☐	☐	☐	☐	☐	
Be creative – come up with new ideas	☐	☐	☐	☐	☐	
Make decisions	☐	☐	☐	☐	☐	
Show confidence	☐	☐	☐	☐	☐	
Communicate well – people understand me	☐	☐	☐	☐	☐	
Think positively	☐	☐	☐	☐	☐	
Take an informed risk	☐	☐	☐	☐	☐	
Solve problems	☐	☐	☐	☐	☐	
Find opportunities	☐	☐	☐	☐	☐	
Make plans and carry them out	☐	☐	☐	☐	☐	
Learn from my mistakes	☐	☐	☐	☐	☐	

Toolkits

About Me (Cont'd)
Rating my level of enterprising skills and attitudes

I can do the following: Name: _____

	Low				High	In what way?
	1	**2**	**3**	**4**	**5**	
Find and use information	☐	☐	☐	☐	☐	
Be organised	☐	☐	☐	☐	☐	
Work with others	☐	☐	☐	☐	☐	
Be co-operative	☐	☐	☐	☐	☐	
Motivate myself and others	☐	☐	☐	☐	☐	
Work independently	☐	☐	☐	☐	☐	
Listen well	☐	☐	☐	☐	☐	
Work hard until I complete a task	☐	☐	☐	☐	☐	
Be reliable	☐	☐	☐	☐	☐	
Be flexible – can change direction when necessary	☐	☐	☐	☐	☐	
Be a leader	☐	☐	☐	☐	☐	

Toolkits

© Enterprising Careers, University of Strathclyde, 2007.

About Another Person

Name: _____

Take 5 minutes to get to know the person that you have been paired with. Find out the things about them that are listed below and write in the answers. Then introduce that person to the rest of your team.

My friend's name is . . .

_____

He/she lives at . . .

_____

His/her favourite food is . . .

_____

His/her favourite TV programme is . . .

_____

His/her favourite pop star is . . .

_____

He/she likes doing . . .

_____

He/she hates doing . . .

_____

He/she is not good at . . .

_____

He/she would like to be better at . . .

_____

If I worked with him/her, I would be able to help with . . .

_____

If I worked with him/her, he/she would be able to help me with . . .

_____

When he/she leaves school he/she would like to . . .

_____

If he/she could change something in the world he/she would change . . .

_____

Toolkits

About Working Together

Name: _____

1. Did you work as a team? _____

2. Did your group work well together? _____

3. Did you make decisions together? _____

4. Did you plan and organise together? _____

5. If there was a problem with the group, how _____
   did you solve it?

_____

6. Who became the leader in your group? _____

7. Why was this person chosen? _____

_____

8. What part did you play in the activity? _____

9. Did you do it well? _____

10. Why? Why not? _____

_____

11. What did others think about your work? _____

_____

12. Tell of a decision you made for the group _____

13. What did you learn about your skills? _____

_____

14. What do you want to learn more about? _____

15. Did you manage your time well? _____

16. If not, what could you have changed? _____

17. If you were to do this again, what would you do _____
    differently next time?

_____

© Enterprising Careers, University of Strathclyde, 2007.

Toolkits

All about My Learning

Rating my Learning   Name _____

		Low 1	2	3	High 4	5
1.	I can organise myself to do my work	☐	☐	☐	☐	☐
2.	I can find answers to things I don't know (asking, Internet, library etc.)	☐	☐	☐	☐	☐
3.	I can work well with others to get the job done	☐	☐	☐	☐	☐
4.	I can be a good leader and help others get the job done	☐	☐	☐	☐	☐
5.	I can be a good listener and follow instructions	☐	☐	☐	☐	☐
6.	I can communicate well with others	☐	☐	☐	☐	☐
7.	I can produce good quality work	☐	☐	☐	☐	☐
8.	I can make sensible decisions	☐	☐	☐	☐	☐
9.	I am a hard worker and keep going till I get the job done	☐	☐	☐	☐	☐
10.	I am very reliable	☐	☐	☐	☐	☐
11.	I am good at coming up with ideas	☐	☐	☐	☐	☐
12.	I like to take responsibility and do not need to be supervised	☐	☐	☐	☐	☐
13.	I am confident	☐	☐	☐	☐	☐
14.	I can make good use of my time	☐	☐	☐	☐	☐
15.	I am normally on time	☐	☐	☐	☐	☐
16.	I am able to make changes if things go wrong	☐	☐	☐	☐	☐
17.	I can usually solve problems	☐	☐	☐	☐	☐

18. Which of the above skills are you best at? _____

19. Which of the above skills would you like to improve? _____

Toolkits

Reflecting on Personal Learning

What have I learned?   Name _____

1.   The thing I most enjoyed about this activity was_____

2.   The most important skill I practised was _____

3.   If I was in charge of the group I would have _____

4.   I was good at _____

5.   One thing I found difficult was _____

6.   I took the lead in _____

7.   I listened and co-operated when _____

8.   I offered ideas for _____

9.   I helped solve a problem when _____

10.   If I had to do this again I would _____

11.   Five things I learned were   1. _____

                                          2. _____

                                          3. _____

                                          4. _____

                                          5. _____

© Enterprising Careers, University of Strathclyde, 2007.

My job

Name: _____

To be completed at the start of the enterprise project.

I think I could help with _____

_____

I would like to _____

To be completed when jobs have been allocated

My job is _____

I got the job by _____

_____

_____

I am happy/not happy about the job I have been asked to do
(cross out the one which does not apply to you)

I feel like this because _____

To be completed at the end of the enterprise.

I feel that I was good/not very good at my job
(cross out the one which does not apply to you)

I think this is because _____

If we run another enterprise I would like to _____

Toolkits

How I felt

Name _____

Read the statements, decide whether you agree or disagree and say why

		Agree	Disagree	My Reasons
1.	I was excited about the thought of running an enterprise.			
2.	I was happy with the role I was allocated.			
3.	I was able to use my particular skills.			
4.	I felt I learned new things.			
5.	I felt I made a real contribution to the enterprise.			
6.	I felt we worked as a good team.			
7.	I was satisfied with our product.			
8.	I would like to run another enterprise.			

Toolkits

Using my skills

Name _____

Write down five skills or interests that you were able to use during the enterprise.

Give examples of when and how they were used.

1.

2.

3.

4.

5.

Toolkits

Teacher Evaluation

Name of Pupil _____

To be completed at the end of the enterprise project.

		Yes	Partly	No
1.	Was clear about his/her role in the enterprise	☐	☐	☐
2.	Took responsibility for part/all of the enterprise	☐	☐	☐
3.	Made use of his/her own particular skills	☐	☐	☐
4.	Contributed to the decision-making process	☐	☐	☐
5.	Was able to help others/teams	☐	☐	☐
6.	Made efforts to co-operate with others	☐	☐	☐
7.	Had a working knowledge of the Business Plan	☐	☐	☐
8.	Was involved in record-keeping	☐	☐	☐
9.	Is aware of the need for market research	☐	☐	☐
10.	Can interpret the results of market research	☐	☐	☐
11.	Readily accepted responsibility	☐	☐	☐
12.	Was motivated by the experience	☐	☐	☐
13.	Learned new skills	☐	☐	☐
14.	Expressed enthusiasm for the enterprise	☐	☐	☐

Toolkits

Working Together

Activities to build skills for working together should be chosen to exemplify or to strengthen a particular theme.

1. Paper Clip Exercise

This demonstrates the benefits of working together – the solutions / options are far greater.

Instructions:

On your own, write down how many ways you can use a paper clip (2 minutes)

Now with a partner, combine your answers (2 minutes).

Is there an increase in the number of your answers?

Now in groups, generate ideas for using paper clips (2 minutes)

How many suggestions have you now?

2. Teambuilding Activity: Building a tower/oil rig

Materials:

4 Newspapers

Sellotape

Can of Coke

2 elastic bands

2 paperclips

Instructions:

Design and make a structure of tower-like proportions, using the materials provided.

From it, you should suspend a full can of Coca Cola in an upright position.

The base of the can must be a minimum height of 210 mm from the base of the structure.

210 mm = the length of the short side of A4 paper.

The winning group will have built a structure which has the greatest distance from the base of the structure to the base of the suspended can.

Toolkits

Team building activity debrief exercise

It is essential that when the pupils have been given the opportunity to participate that they are allowed the time and encouraged to think about the part they played and where their strengths and weaknesses lie.

Encourage them to consider their performance in the following areas.

- **Teamwork**

  Did you participate / lead / listen / co-operate / negotiate / suggest?

- **Planning**

  What part did you play in the planning process?

- **Organisation**

  How did you participate on the task?

- **What would you do differently next time?**

Toolkits

How to Enterprise a Lesson

Developing a more enterprising approach in the classroom

When planning a lesson, ask yourself some of the following questions.

A: in your classroom:

1. How can I **share responsibility** for learning by allowing the pupils to make more decisions and participate in their learning?

2. How can I make this **real/ relevant** to the world outside of the classroom?

3. How can I **encourage group activities** allowing the pupils to learn with and from one another and assume **roles** within the groups?

4. How can I **work with other adults** from within and outwith the school and build **relationships and** partnerships?

5. How can I encourage **pupils to reflect on their learning**, learning how to learn?

B: With your colleagues:

- How can I contribute to the School Development Plan?

- How can I move things forward in my Department or Faculty?

Use the template overleaf to consider a lesson or topic which you currently deliver, and think about how you might take a more enterprising approach. The final page of the template allows you to reflect on the impact of the change in approach.

Toolkits

Enterprising Teacher
Planning a lesson
Subject:

Lesson/ Topic:

How you usually deliver it:

How you might change your approach and "Enterprise" it!

1. By encouraging pupils to take **responsibility/make decisions**

2. Putting learning into a **REAL context** – challenge/experience – **action**

3. Learning with and from one another – **roles/risks**

4. Involving partners in learning – **building relationships**
    (Business / Community / Parents / Families / other adults in school)

5. Formative assessment input – **review and reflect**

Discussing and learning from others (pairs and group work)

Changes I may now consider

Others I may involve in my teaching

Toolkits

Implementing an enterprising approach

Impact on me as teacher and learner:

Impact on pupils as learners

Moving forward, I will . . .

© Enterprising Careers, University of Strathclyde, 2007.

Toolkits

Moving Forward in Enterprise in Education

Toolkit

Where are you and where do you want to be?

The following is a development tool to assist you in your school to look at your current provision for Enterprise in Education and consider how this might be developed.

Having gone through the process you should be able to make a judgement on actions to be taken and gaps to be addressed.

Toolkits

1. **Answer the following questions to outline your enterprise in education provision.**

Question	Currently	Action required
What documents in the school outline the provision of E in E? Audit / policy / plan		
Who is involved in developing the unique identity of the school and sharing its vision?		
Who manages E in E in your school?		
Do the school staff have an agreed vision / understanding of E in E?		
How are staff in the school encouraged to take an enterprising approach?		
How are resources used to support E in E?		
Does the ethos in your school support enterprising behaviours?		
How many of your staff are trained to deliver an enterprise approach?		
How does the school support CPD in E in E?		
How many cross-curricular enterprise activities are provided annually?		
How many staff establish external links to make the curriculum relevant?		
What percentage of your staff use an enterprising approach in their classroom? How often?		
What stand alone – externally produced - enterprise activities does your school provide?		

Toolkits

Question	Current	Action required
What stand alone – internally developed - enterprise activities does your school provide?		
What instances are there of pupils participating in school organisation?		
To what degree is the curriculum relevant to the needs of your pupils?		
What can you do to increase the relevance of the school curriculum?		
How often do the pupils go out on organised visits to link with the world of work/careers?		
How many external partners support the school in E in E? How often per year?		
What partnership agreements are in existence to assist in enhancing the curriculum?		
How does your school work with and reflect the positive values of the local community though E in E?		
How does your school encourage links with parents and families through E in E?		
How often in a year does each pupil experience E in E approach?		
Are you using QI's for E in E as a self evaluation tool?		

Toolkits

2. Complete a SWOT analysis of your school in relation to enterprise in education.

Strengths	Weaknesses
Opportunities	**Threats**

Underline or highlight the two most significant in each category

Toolkits

Section 5

Enterprising Careers – What we can do for you

Useful Website Addresses

Enterprising Careers - Mission Statement:

The Centre for Studies in Enterprise, Career Development and Work was created in 2003 to encourage evidence-based policy and practice in enterprise in education, career development and work-related learning.

Events
Conferences
Our National Conference, which takes place annually in March, provides strategies to move forward on Enterprise in Education.

The themes focus on current, innovative good practice.

Seminars
Early evening seminars, held at Jordanhill campus, will be of interest to all those involved in Enterprise in Education – topics and speakers of interest.

Local and National Events
To meet the demands of a growing market, the Centre offers events on specific themes, the most recent being:
- 5 Countries Conference
- Exhibition by business providers supporting Enterprise in Education

Publications
Packs
- Enterprising Infants- resource material to support enterprise activity in P1- 3 (ages 5-8)
- Go for Enterprise – resource material to support enterprise activity in P4-7 (ages 8-12)
- Up for Enterprise – resource material to support enterprise activity in S1/S2 (ages 12-14)

Books
- *Excellence in Enterprise* – resource material enabling pupils, teachers and whole school to evaluate enterprise projects
- *The Enterprising School-* implementation tool with material to support schools in developing an enterprising approach.
- *The Role of Parents and Families in Enterprise in Education* – discussion paper
- *Quality Awards for Enterprise Education-* discussion paper
- *Enterprising Ideas for Secondary Schools* 2007 – implementation tool
- *Enterprising Ideas for Primary Schools* – coming soon – implementation tool

Resources

Enterprise

The Centre provides wide-ranging activities relating to enterprise education.

CPD opportunities

One day courses for classroom assistants, teachers, SMT, cluster groups and local authority staff can be customised to suit particular needs. These include:

The Enterprising Teacher
The Enterprising School
Enterprising Learning Assistants
The Enterprise Umbrella
Excellence in Enterprise

Initial Teacher Education As part of the Faculty of Education at the University, we offer Enterprise in Education modules in both the Bachelor of Education (Hons) and the Professional Graduate Diploma in Education courses – Primary and Secondary - in Enterprise in Education.

Chartered Teacher programme: The team offers an option module as part of this course.

Postgraduate Certificate/Diploma in Enterprise in Education. This course continues to attract a number of students from a range of backgrounds. All aspects of Enterprise in Education are addressed.

Recent research and evaluation activities include such topics as:
- *'Part-time Employment of Pupils'*
- *'Inclusive Enterprise Education'*
- *'The Enterprising School'*
- *'The Role of Parents and Families in Enterprise Education'*
- *'Employability'*
- *'Transition Resources for Young People'*
- *'Preparing School Leavers for the World of Work'*
- *'Labour Market Information and Career Decision Making'.*

Evaluations of particular projects and programmes are regularly undertaken on behalf of stakeholders.

Partnership with a wide range of national organisations includes planning, supporting and delivering innovative programmes for business and education. We are also currently working with educationalists in England, Ireland, Netherlands, Sweden, Finland, Australia, Estonia, China, Japan, Malawi and Zambia.

Resources

Career Guidance

Academic Qualifications

MSc / Diploma / Certificate in Careers Guidance and Development
This course is intended mainly for students who wish to become career guidance practitioners. It includes study of the labour market, education and training policies, career theory and professional skills development.

Research and Consultancy
We have a strong profile in research and evaluation of career related issues providing a service at various levels from school departments to policy makers. We work in partnership with a number of professional bodies addressing the development of Determined to Succeed, strand 4 – appropriately focused career education.

Resources
The Centre is involved in the development of a number of career education resources with other partners.

Work Related Learning

The Centre is involved in research and in carrying out evaluations of education for work and related projects. We provide CPD opportunities for subject teachers and school managers.

One-day Industry Courses for Teachers
The Centre provides industry based courses for subject teachers covering many syllabus topics. We link with a wide range of businesses and organisations to help teachers update their skills and knowledge related to their subject. A course will typically provide information about the industrial host's products and processes which have subject syllabus relevance, provide career information which can be passed on to students and engage teachers in practical activity which can be replicated in the classroom.

Subjects covered

Art & Design	Geography	Mathematics	Physics
Biology/Biotech	Graphic Communication	Modern Languages	Product Design
Business Education	Guidance/Personal Dev	Modern Studies	Travel & Tourism
Chemistry	Home Economics	Music	Interview Skills

Do you need support for Enterprise in Education?

Enterprising Careers, part of the Faculty of Education at the University of Strathclyde, works with local authorities, school cluster groups and individual schools to help prepare our young people for life.

As an internationally-renowned independent centre, we run customised programmes for professionals involved in Enterprise in Education (EiE) at all levels.

We offer:
- training and support for EiE officers in local authorities and schools
- courses for headteachers and senior management teams on leadership, change management, culture change and policy development in EiE
- whole-school sessions on The Enterprising School
- resource-based courses for teachers
- courses for support staff
- industry awareness courses for teachers
- support for businesses and community groups working with schools
- awareness-raising sessions for parents and families.

Contact Linda Brownlow, Co-director, to discuss customised support.

Centre for Studies in Enterprise Career Development and Work
University of Strathclyde, Jordanhill Campus
Southbrae Drive
Glasgow
G13 1PP
tel: 0141 950 3141   fax: 0141 950 3919

e-mail: enterprising.careers@strath.ac.uk
www.strath.ac.uk/enterprisingcareers

THE PLACE OF USEFUL LEARNING

Useful Web Addresses

www.businesslink.gov.uk
Advisory Service for Business

www.bitc.org.uk
Business in the Community

www.bgateway.com
Scottish Enterprise Business Gateway

www.can-online.org.uk/se
Community Action Network for social enterprise

www.careers-scotland.org.uk
Enterprise in Education support

www.cbi.org.uk
CBI

www.cets.coop
Co-op Educational Trust Scotland (CETS)

www.scottishchambers.org.uk
Chambers of Commerce

www.ccea.org.uk
Council for Curriculum, Examinations and Assessment, N Ireland

www.dest.gov.au/schools/enterprise
Australian Govt, Dept of Educ, Science and Training

www.determinedtosucceed.co.uk
"Determined to Succeed is the Scottish Executive's strategy for enterprise in education with the aim of helping Scotland's young people develop self-confidence, self-belief and the determination to succeed in life and work"

www.entreva.net
Enterprise Education training in Australia

www.fairtrade.org.uk
Fairtrade organisations

www.fsb.org.uk
Federation of Small Businesses

www.fsmed.org/group4.asp
Durham University – Enterprise Education

Resources

www.futureskillsscotland.org.uk
Scottish Enterprise/Highlands & Islands Enterprise

www.hmie.gov.uk/documents/publicaions/hgiosqueie.html
Quality Indicators for Enterprise in Education

www.keepscotlandbeautiful.org
ECO schools and other ideas

www.ltscotland.org.uk
Support for better learning

www.nebpn.org
The National Education Business Partnership Network

www.nfea.com
The National Federation of Enterprise Agencies

www.parentzonescotland.gov.uk
Involving parents in the education of their children

www.psybt.org.uk
The Prince's Scottish Youth Business Trust

www.princes-trust.org.uk
The Prince's Trust

www.sbs.gov.uk
Small Business Service

www.scotland.gov.uk
Curriculum for Excellence; Ambitious, Excellent Schools

www.sbcscot.com
Scottish Business in the Community

www.sfeu.ac.uk
The Scottish Further Education Unit

www.sqa.org.uk
Scottish Qualifications Authority

www.ssec.org.uk
Scottish Social Enterprise

www.strath.ac.uk/enterprisingcareers
Centre for Studies in Enterprise, Career Development & Work

www.teachernet.gov.uk/teachingandlearning/14to19/ks4/enterpriseeducation
Enterprise Education for Schools in England

www.young-enterprise.org.uk
Young Enterprise - range of programmes in Enterprise Education

Resources